Note to Readers

If you've ever felt lost as a mother, a woman, a girl. If you've felt oceans of sadness—not just your own, but a generations' worth. If you've fucked around and found out, then please keep reading. CW for violence against women and animals. As much as I wish this memoir didn't contain either, it's an unfortunate fact in intimate partner violence and relationships of all kinds, not just romantic. Do take care of your heads and hearts. For more information, please visit The National Center on Domestic Violence, Trauma, & Mental Health at http://www.nationalcenterdvtraumamh.org/.

When we seek out saviors, we eventually discover the fairytales were all wrong, the needle of the spindle is too dull to prick, the perfect king and queen parents stopped looking for their stolen daughter. The princes were blinded in their quests and lost themselves in magical forests forever. The real quest and moral of the stories were never in these tales. We have to save ourselves. But sometimes, someone comes along and helps you out. Sometimes that person is your friend, a family member, a partner. Sometimes it's an ocean. A child.

All names and some places have been changed in order to protect privacy (and so I don't get sued). Other businesses and locations have been kept true to their names because they play a loving role in this timeline.

AURA

HILLARY LEFTWICH

Future Tense Books
Portland, Oregon

'

AURA: A Memoir
Copyright © 2022 Hillary Leftwich

Hollywood: Originally published as "Divination" in Stockholm Literary Review, 2019
Dorothy: Originally "The Wizard of Oz Snowglobe," published in Matter Press, 2016

Paperback ISBN: 978-1-892061-93-5
Limited Edition Hardcover ISBN: 978-1-892061-92-8

Edited by Kevin Sampsell and Emma Alden.
Layout by Michael Kazepis.
Cover art by Sarah Best: Symbiosis (Mixed media, collage, sculpted paper).
Cover design by Michael J. Seidlinger.

First edition. Printed in the United States of America.

Published by Future Tense Books.
www.futuretensebooks.com
Portland, Oregon

For my son. To the moon and the stars and back again.

Who defined me? My culture, a culture of mercy, a living codex. I am
a unique culture of one, from everywhere. I am her map and her self.
I am everyone in the story; I am the story.
        —Alice Notley

They say I am protected from harm
Because the Virgin Mary put her heel
Upon a snake's head and crushed it
For the sake of all pregnant women.
I am safe, I say to myself and pray for mercy
        —Ai Ogawa

If you remember me, then I don't care if everyone else forgets.
        —Haruki Murakami

I wish the sun was the moon instead
        —C Leftwich

au·ra

The distinctive atmosphere or quality that seems to surround and be generated by a person, thing, or place.

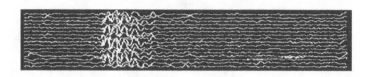

There is a page dedicated to firsts in your baby book—first smile, two months old. First laugh, three months old, First rolling over, four months old. You sat up at six months old. You were crawling at five months old. Your first steps were on Easter day, 2005. Your first words were "Da-Da" at eight months old. And displayed behind a clear laminate page is your tiny red medical alert bracelet with the word *Epilepsy* engraved on the front. There were many firsts that I might forget without your baby book to remind me. But our journey together will never be forgotten, even if you don't remember most of it to this day, just scattered remnants that come and go through your brain like the seizures that ravaged you for years.

Some things, Son, are worth abandoning, and some things, even though we try, can never be forgotten. There is a difference between abandonment and forgetting. Remember that one is an act of power.

There's a letter I wrote to you in your baby book shortly after you were born. When I read it, I'm reminded of hope. A hope that my love for you will support you in a world that is often cruel. But within this cruelty, life manages to redeem itself within certain spaces. I am writing this for you because we are still here, able to witness all of its ugliness and grace combined. Remember, we can always go back to another beginning. And beginnings, Son, can be terrifying, but sometimes they can be beautiful.

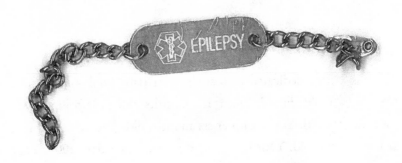

What Men Do

Once, before I knew you were growing inside me, I planned to escape your father and move to Seattle. *Seattle.* The word evokes images of cold, icy waters and the smell of damp moss. I never told anyone of my plans, but if I had, they would be curious about my choice of location across the country. I read about Seattle in books I checked out from the library. How it was named after Chief Si'ahl of the Duwamish and Suquamish tribes. How cold green waters bound the land. I mouthed the name over and over, *Seattle.* It's a spell I can't speak out loud.

Maggie, my bank representative, assured me my application was approved, but they needed a reason for the loan. She sounded surprised when I told her Seattle. "It's beautiful there, but very rainy. It can be quite depressing if you aren't used to it." I recall how your father grabbed my cat by the back of her neck and threw her in the bathroom one night. I heard the electric razor switch on and the buzz as he shaved all her fur off. How she cried out in pain. I knew if I tried to save her, he would make me pay.

The Suquamish and Duwamish tribes called Seattle their home long before the Denny Party traveled across the ocean on a boat named *Exact*, led by Arthur Denny, and descended upon their land before stealing everything from them. There's a picture of Arthur Denny in the library book I'm reading, a dead stare in his eyes. It's a look that never faltered as he took everything that didn't belong to him, disregarding their culture, their language, their lives. He erased them. That's what men do. They erase.

In 1993, when I was a sophomore in high school, the singer Mia Zapata from the punk band The Gits was discovered murdered on the street in Seattle. Her bruised body was found abandoned on the road. Left for the crows to peck at. I was fascinated by Mia's death in the way teenage girls are held captive by a strong, older woman whose life has ended. I held her words close, knowing there would be no more. I read how Mia's father described her as living in two different worlds. One where she wanted to be someone, and one where there was no meaning for her. I thought about Mia lying in the middle of a road, already dead, her body posed in a mock crucifixion as the crows circled, the sound of the late-night bar crowds slowly ceasing. How there were two sides of the street on either side of her. How she was left in the middle, but not by choice. A man came. Overtook her. Took her. Then killed her, his name eluding the police for almost a decade, Mia's name and legacy slowly fading. That's what men do. They take.

One day, Son, you will grow up and be a man too. But I hope you will come to know the difference between taking and giving. Between erasing and inclusion.

A Spell for Mothers and Daughters

Mothers: Take your daughter's hair in your hands and begin the braiding ritual. This binds their hair to their bodies and their souls.

Mama braids my hair after bathtime and before bed. A soothing smell of lavender lotion and sweet soap nestles the air. She sings to me about horses and cowboys. Wildfires and women. I ask her to sing the song about the lost horse, about the woman who dies looking for him. His name was Wildfire, she tells me, cooing his name over and over. Did the horses die, Mama? Sssh, she rocks me in her warm arms and whispers:

Just because we try to save someone doesn't mean it always ends in tragedy.

Mean Girls

Hell is a teenage girl. —Anita *"Needy" Lesnicky,* JENNIFER'S BODY

Before I knew about men, I knew about girls first. Girls in all their pre-teen and teen transformative states of confusion, madness, and hilarity. Fifth grade proved to be a pivotal moment of pre-teen terror in my life. Before, elementary life was easy, predictable. But after fourth grade, something turned wild in the once complacent girls in my class once fifth grade began. Something that smelled primitive and dark. I recall smelling this same scent on myself, but I'd always had this scent on me, long before I caught whiff of it on anyone else. It was the smell of dank earth and stagnant waters.

I spent nearly every day trying not to get my ass kicked by one or more of the girls-turned-rabid in my class. One month, in particular, proved to be exceptionally difficult. After a new girl named Janna transferred to our class from Minnesota midway through the year, she became the target of Veronica and April, the two girls no one wanted to be noticed by, let alone be the target of their senseless vengefulness. But if I wasn't in their line of fire, I usually managed to scrape by under their radar, then I was either with them or against them, according to their fifth-grade logic. After witnessing Veronica and April sabotage Janna on her way home from school one day, throwing rocks at her and calling her slut, whore, Minnesota Mama's Girl, and trailer trash hooker, I knew their usual antics of name-calling and social humiliation at the monkey bars had become a whole new level of bullying. Veronica and April had become what I later witnessed in pop culture movies thanks to Hollywood: The two Heathers from Heathers, the Nancy Downs from The Craft, the Regina George, and Gretchen Wieners from Means Girls. I stood frozen on the sidewalk, halfway between 7-Eleven and my dad's apartment, gripping the straps to my pink backpack until my fingers lost feeling. They both saw me; Janna saw me, but I did nothing to intervene. It was too late. Veronica and April now knew I knew, and I had two choices: keep my mouth shut or tell an adult. Either choice had terrible consequences.

Veronica's dad was rumored to be part of the Satanic Church and looked suspiciously like James Brolin from Amityville Horror. Had I been older, I would have found him attractive, but I only found him terrifying at that age. April was stout and built like a wrestler. Myths from the playground circulated that she had kicked the asses of several junior high school girls for giving her the side-eye at Baskin-Robbins. When it came to ratting them out, I kept my mouth shut. It was a decision I wasn't proud of, but necessary for self-preservation. I managed to avoid Veronica and April the entire school year, hoping they wouldn't return the following year by some miracle.

But after fifth grade, the summer before my sixth-grade year, things changed. Within those few months, Veronica and I started to practice witchcraft together. How I even found myself mixed up with Veronica was a fluke, something I had no intention of ever doing, until we stumbled into each other at the local library in the spiritualism and religion aisle. She was alone, and without April by her side, she acted less like she had to prove something, dropping her guard when she was alone with me without her sidekick. One section was devoted to Wicca—what most witchcraft was called back then— which covered such a broad topic but still interesting enough to lure two girls on the same day while looking for the exact same subject. Manitou Springs was within walking distance, a conglomerate of hippie new-age types mixed in with the artistic community and several Indigenous store owners. These different influences provided a unique haven in its own slice of Colorado Springs. Lucky for us, it provided plenty of books on the subject of Wiccan practices and folk magic.

At first, it was something fun and mysterious that I explored by myself, but now I had Veronica to share it with. Like most grade school relationships, friendships were fleeting and often lasted or ended based on temporary allegiance or a common interest. Alone, I would do simple charms and spells; Make My Brother Stop Being a Douchebag or Make My Parents Fall in Love Again and Not Be Divorced. Things I knew reciting words in the flickering of a candle could never change. Still, it gave me a little bit of power in a world where I felt I had no stability. Veronica and I made it a routine to go to the library and check out books on spells, magic, and the ancient ways of witches. Before hanging out with Veronica, I assembled an altar in my closet, hidden away from my dad and my brother's prying eyes. I stared at drawings of women in black hats riding on broomsticks and leaning over bubbling cauldrons filled with smoke. But more than just the depictions of witches and witchcraft, we dug deep into the spellwork itself. The rituals and incantations. How to cast a spell. How to charge a ward. All of these became scripture to us, our own religion. We took it and ourselves very seriously. Magick, at the time, was a way to have control over something when my life felt like it was out of control.

☿

One Saturday, when Veronica was spending the night, she brought up the subject of demons. It was the weekend my brother and I stayed at my dad's apartment, the other times we stayed with our mom. After the divorce, we spent one week at Mom's house and one week at Dad's apartment until the routine became too much for everyone, and we decided to stay only on the weekends. We lived out of our suitcases, never feeling fully settled. Our belongings were packed hastily in mismatched bags and cardboard boxes.

I think about how this impacted my life as an adult, how I never wanted that kind of life for you, but it's how we both wound up living—always moving. *Remember when I said never to close a door without knowing how to open it? Sometimes, Son, when you try to make a better life than your childhood, the past is all you know. My life was a suitcase. All I knew was to keep moving. Never unpack.*

"Write this down," Veronica tells me, handing me a piece of paper and pointing at a paragraph from one of our books we checked out from the library that day. I stared at the sentence and shook my head.

"This doesn't have anything to do with witchcraft," I tell her.

I was only twelve, but I knew from all the books I was reading that black magic was not something you messed with, especially as a kid. I was used to practicing simple spells from books that were gentle with words and intentions. Spells that I was able to tailor to my own pre-teen wants, such as getting a secret crush to like me back or spells to make myself more popular.

"Do it, or I'll make your life a living hell. You know I will."

Her eyes were black like her hair, which was straight and thick and fell to her waist. She was the same age as me but already had the body of a teenager. Her breasts had developed in the fourth grade, and she started her period later that year. I was still flat as a board and didn't see puberty hitting me for years. I was okay with that. The way the boys at school and the men out in public stared at Veronica, I wouldn't know how to handle that kind of attention. She handed me a pen and pointed at the paper. I sighed, knowing if I didn't do what she told me, life at school would be hell. I thought of Janna and the rocks thrown at her pale, thin body. I thought of eating lunch alone and spending recess avoiding everyone by the monkey bars, the place where shit always went down. I didn't want to write what Veronica wanted me to write, but I had no other choice. Picking up the pen, I wrote down the sentence and laid the pen back down on the paper where my words were now written.

"Now, we recite it three times while holding hands, but first, let's light this candle." She took a box of matches out of her pink hoodie pocket and lit the dark purple candle I had on my dresser, carrying it like a glass of water filled too full. Setting it down in front of us, she locked eyes with me and grabbed my hand.

"Say it," she squeezed my hands harder.

"I love Satan," I began softly, not wanting my brother to hear us between the thin walls of our apartment. "Louder," Veronica demanded, putting more pressure on my hands. "I love Satan," I said louder, and she joined in after me. "I always will. I'll love Satan until I rot in Hell." We repeated the chant three more times, each time louder until my brother pounded on the wall next to us. Veronica let go of my hands and smiled. "Good. Now I won't have to kick your ass at school in front of everyone."

A Spell to Protect Your Childhood

Use a small stuffed doll to serve as your body. Take a few strands of your hair, cut a small section out of the doll, and place your hair inside. Write your name on a piece of paper three times to symbolize your past, present, and future. Fold the paper into a tiny square and place it inside the doll, securing it with a safety pin or sewing back in place.

I wrapped my Raggedy Ann doll in a plastic bag and hid her body behind the six-month-old package of ground beef that sat in our freezer and would never be eaten. Frozen, to freeze. A state born within the form of water. Water ignites images of cleansing, purity. Used in baptisms to cleanse the soul. A purification.

One day, I would want my childhood back.

Save Yourself for That Man

When I thought about starting this memoir out with my childhood, I had an immediate reaction of resistance. So much of my childhood feels dirty, secretive. But some aspects are important to face within this memoir, including my early relationships, especially with girls. This includes Angela. She was my best friend since the first grade. Somehow, she managed to stay under the radar and avoid the bullying from Veronica and April and their followers. Maybe it was because her stepdad was rich, and she found ways to buy herself protection by offering small gifts—the good lunches she brought to school and money for mall shopping. She was offering a form of mafia-like bribery in exchange for being left alone. Angela's older sister Renee graduated from Christian School of Colorado, CSC, and was engaged to her high school sweetheart, Ryan. This meant Angela enrolled at the same school to start junior high and avoid the public school system. I knew if I continued to the junior high my section of town designated me to attend along with Veronica and April, I would have to continuously balance protecting myself with appeasing the two of them.

Ever since the night we invoked Satan in my tiny bedroom, I didn't want anything else to do with Veronica. That following weekend, my dad had found our demon-summoning chant on my altar in my closet (a place he was forbidden to look for that very reason) and told me Veronica was not allowed over again as he shook his head in either disbelief or disappointment, I couldn't tell which. I imagined this had to be one thing he was not prepared to handle as a parent. I was relieved but pretended to act annoyed and bitter anyway because I didn't want him to know the full extent of Veronica's wrath. It wasn't the demonic summoning that bothered me. It was the fact that she was trying to control me while simultaneously ruining my life. The little things she did spoke volumes about her power over me and our newfound friendship. Lending outfits was a common practice amongst friends, but Veronica always returned my clothes covered in bleach stains if she returned them at all.

"I accidentally spilled bleach on them when I was washing them. Sorry." She would say, flipping her hair back. "Those shorts are terrible anyway. Where'd you buy them? Kmart?"

Other times, my belongings would suddenly disappear. At first, I blamed my older brother, but every time Veronica left my apartment, something in my room wound up missing. A small pewter figurine of a unicorn, a pair of socks with black hearts. A bubble gum flavored lip gloss.

Pink plastic unicorn-shaped earrings Angela had given me for my birthday.

☿

Time operates differently when you're a kid. I factored everything based on seasons, specifically summer and fall. Fall in Colorado is when the aspens begin to turn, shedding the green shades of their leaves and changing to hues of copper, gold, and sunburnt orange. When the school year ended, I was ready for fall, which meant getting away from Veronica and her group of followers and out from under their regime. Our witchcraft sessions that once were fun and filled with excitement and wonder had turned dark and filled with power plays, mainly on Veronica's part. She used the rumors that her dad was a member of The Satanic Church (which, back then, in a conservative Christian town, was the absolute worst) to hold seniority over me, telling me she knew more than I did, and I should be learning from her. I wanted more than anything to take back my self-worth, knowing that what I was still learning and practicing had nothing to do with power plays. But the immature, self-conscious girl inside of me didn't care. I wanted Veronica to back the fuck off. I spent nights throwing Tarot cards to see my future without her friendship. I cast protection spells and eased my way into binding spells over Veronica I learned about in the books I continued to check out from the library until one day, all of the books were gone. When I asked the librarian where they were, she said they were stolen, and they wouldn't be ordering more for the time being. I was dumbfounded. It had to be Veronica that stole the books, cutting my only tie to learning more and possibly even protecting myself. I kept pulling The Devil card over and over when trying to gain insight into Veronica's plans. I knew any kind of witchcraft I wanted to learn couldn't be the kind where it involved trying to screw with someone over something petty. There had to be more action to break away from Veronica's spell over me.

I avoided Veronica and April the final few months of school, ignoring phone calls and dodging down different ways home to avoid being sabotaged. I decided there was no way in hell I was going to the same junior high as the Two *Heathers*. The Two *Mean Girls*. With Nancy from *The Craft*. I was scared and they could smell the fear on me like an injured animal.

You're dead, fuckface! They hollered at me from across the road, threatening to jump me. Veronica flashed a butcher knife from her kitchen, one I'd seen her use to cut bologna sandwiches in half while hanging out at her apartment the few times I was invited. The same knife she told me her dad used in his Satanic rituals. I ran as fast as I could, my backpack bumping against my back as I sprinted from sidewalk to parking lot and finally made it to my apartment building, bursting into the door as my brother jumped from his seat on the couch, TV blaring *Loony Toons*.

"The fuck is wrong with you?" I ignored him and ran to my room, slamming the door behind me, peeking out the window to see if they followed me home. My brother was of zero help. He left my battles for me to fight, not once offering to put in a hand to scare them all off. He was older and had connections. He could have said something to save his little sister. The only interactions with my brother back then were playing defense to his older brother torture: shaving all my doll's hair into mohawks, turning my doorknob the other way around, so he locked me inside of my bedroom. And the summer we stayed at Mom's house, he moved most of my stuff from my bedroom into the rusted-out tool shed in the backyard and told me Mom kicked me out as punishment for eating all of the Lucky Charms cereal.

I'd seen Veronica and her helpers jump other girls and even a few boys before. They didn't fuck around. Even girls in junior high were scared of Veronica. Rumors were floating around our class, people whispering behind my back, rumors that Angela finally told me about. It confirmed what I had been worried about for months, just waiting for the truth to come out that what I believed was something small had been blown entirely out of proportion.

"They want to tie you up and leave you in the abandoned building at the end of the road by our school," Angela told me during lunch one day. "Even worse, slit your throat and leave you for dead." She handed me her bag of Cheetos as if to reassure me. But nothing could make me feel safe again. I couldn't sleep at night worrying about what would happen to me if I went to the same junior high as everyone else in my class. They knew my routes home—even the secret ones. How all of our parents were divorced, we had no adult supervision and knew I was an open target, and they could get away with anything they wanted to. The only way I knew to save myself was to change schools or move away, and only one was a viable option.

I spent the summer convincing my mom and my dad to send me to the school Angela was going to. CSC. Christian School of Colorado. It wasn't easy getting them to agree on anything after their divorce years before. My brother and I had been spending the majority of our childhood being shuffled back and forth from our mom's rental house to our dad's apartment, rotating schedules and sometimes choosing one over the other if it was more convenient. Sometimes my brother got mad at my mom and would stay with my dad and vice versa. Angela's childhood was far more stable than mine, and her attending CSC, a private school, was her ticket into a whole new life, new classmates, and a guarantee to never see any of the kids in our class as we all moved on to the seventh grade and junior high. She could completely reinvent herself. I could too.

I argued with my parents that I was worried about Veronica and wanted to go to school with my best friend. I reminded my dad of the Satan chant he had discovered and how Veronica would be in my same class again. Since the second grade, Angela and I had been inseparable, yet we were complete opposites. She had long, dark curly hair and was every boy's crush in our elementary school. I was awkward and skinny and hid behind my waist-length hair. My idols on TV and movies at the time were also the exact opposite of me: Sigourney Weaver, Wonder Woman, Pam Grier, Carrie Fisher, Janet Jackson, She-Ra, Tina Turner. Still, I found solace in the strength of these women, even if I never felt the same strength myself.

Neither of my parents was religious, though my dad found religion fascinating and enjoyed learning about all its forms. He knew more about the doctrines of Christ than any typical Christian. Knowing what I know now, this fact seems even more commonplace than it had as a child. With all of my might and intent, I spent the summer wearing my parents down separately, casting spells with candles, the words *I will attend CSC* carved into the bodies of the candles I burned every week, a new offering made with every new candle lit. In hindsight, the intention and manner I was using to get into the school were ridiculous, but at the time, it felt like my only chance.

Still, it was a surprise when they somehow managed to come up with the money to pay the tuition, allowing me to go. I still don't know how. My parents claimed to have talked to Angela's mom and stepdad to get more information, and I'm not sure if they worked out some kind of loan with them. My mom and dad both worked low-paying jobs and had to raise two kids separately, both on a shared custody agreement. Angela's stepdad and mom didn't have to worry about money. They lived in a huge house on High Bank Drive, part of the wealthy neighborhood, and owned a ranch with a ton of land somewhere in the mountains. Her stepdad sold real estate while her mom stayed at home, chain-smoking cigarettes and popping her gum while thumbing through beauty and lifestyle magazines. But she wasn't entirely selfish. She paid her best friend to clean their house once a week. Angela's stepdad was unrelenting about his decision not to allow her to attend a public school.

"No daughter of mine is going to a public junior high," he told us over dinner one night at her house. "Public school is where all the sluts and losers go." He looked at Angela's mom, who rolled her eyes, then he looked at us, pointing with his fork still holding a chunk of the steak–cooked rare–he had just cut. "Find yourselves a good man to marry. Save yourself for that man." He popped the piece of pink steak into his mouth, chewing loudly. "You don't want to wind up pregnant living in a trailer park, do you, girls?"

Years later, the image of living in a trailer park and all its classist and sexist implications always led me back to think of Angela and Angela's stepdad. How men in my childhood, both in real life and on TV, made me believe I needed a man to save me from my own path to destruction. They used specific wording, phrases, and imagery to evoke a sense of fear, and from that fear, the only action was to allow me to be saved by a man. It didn't sit right with me, and for years I pictured my dad and mom asking for help from Angela's parents to send me to CSC because they couldn't afford it on their own. I didn't know then that parents sometimes have to lose their pride to do what they think is best for their kids. I could never imagine that by changing the typical narrative in my life as a child and teenager, I was romanticizing a situation that would later come to pass in my own life. One that was far from the strong female icons and movie stars I idolized.

Let Me Save You and Fuck You

When I was eight years old, I watched a documentary on TV about Jim Jones, a pastor and cult leadaer, not understanding why hundreds of bodies were lying on the ground. Dead dogs, tails stiff in the air. Children with their mouths caught open, oral syringes stained bright red from Kool-Aid mix laying next to them. The camera pans from bodies to more bodies, switching to a clip of Jones raising his fists, God flying from his lips "Oh Lord Oh Lord Oh Lord!" I didn't know one man could have that much control over so many people. I felt sick.

"Cult mentality," my dad said, shaking his head. "When you brainwash a group of people, they no longer have their individual beliefs or thoughts." He knew this situation and others well. Despite growing up in small-town Indiana, my dad found himself entrenched in the horrors of his generation: Vietnam, Civil Rights protests, and the anti-war movements.

Years later, in my late teens/early twenties, I visited Waco, Texas, with a boyfriend who would become my first husband. His father lived in Waco, and he wanted to see him, so we drove 13 hours from Colorado through the panhandle with no stops in the middle of summer. The temperature jumped from the upper 80's to 100 degrees with 90 percent humidity. For a Colorado-born girl, I was not in my element. I came down quickly with heat exhaustion and stayed cooped up in the tiny air-conditioned home his father lived in as much as possible. Still, we wound up getting lost as an adventure to get away from the house and stumbled on the burnt remains of The Branch Davidians Compound.

The Waco Massacre happened in 1993 during the spring of my sophomore year in high school. I remember watching the devastation detonate on live TV as the FBI set the Waco compound on fire. For almost two months, the entire country was privy to the showdown between the cult leader David Koresh, the ATF, and the FBI. A UPS driver delivered a package to The Branch when it broke open, exposing firearms and black powder. The driver alerted the local police, who immediately got the federal government involved, and a weapons search warrant by the ATF, nicknamed "Showtime," quickly followed. For days, weeks, and months, the everyday lives of The Branch and David Koresh were televised live for the nation to witness like an episode of Jerry Springer. Here is David, playing his guitar like some kind of rock god—bushy, early '90s rock dad hair blowing in the hot Waco breeze as he pumped his body into his electric guitar. Here are the Branch members, going about their daily lives in routines familiar to them and those watching; chores, schooling, children playing. The fact that all of this was televised in real-time was even more bizarre, giving America an unaccustomed glimpse into what the news had deemed a "Christian cult." People from nearby towns sold "Christian Cult" T-shirts with the Mt. Carmel compound images on the front. Curious tourists flooded Waco to get a glimpse of the showdown when the images being flashed on TV weren't enough. The ATF and FBI fired at the windows of the compound, blasting loud music, odd chanting, and the recorded screams of rabbits being slaughtered at all hours of the night and day, tanks running into the sides of the building, and eventually, a fire broke out that started the massacre of 76 Branch Davidians and the death of four federal agents. During those months, I had dreams about the standoff and David Koresh. In one dream, I was one of David Koresh's wives. I wore a modest white dress with tiny light blue flowers, and my hair had come undone from its bun. David was hiding in the tunnels underneath the compound. In my dream, he was alive, urging me to come down further into the tunnels with him, to run away and join him where no one would know us, and we could begin a new life. The next day, David Koresh's body was found with a bullet in his brain.

Pulling up to the remains of the compound felt as if we were witnessing a crime scene. There was barely anything left of the building aside from a few concrete slabs. To the right, the school bus that had transported the members to and from excursions stood empty, the tires blown and melted. Further down, in a field all by itself, stood David Koresh's prized motorcycle, still standing on its kickstand, the body burnt, making it inoperable. I was surprised to still see vehicles there two years after the massacre. On our way out, an old woman whose shack we had passed on the way in, thinking it was abandoned, flagged us down. She came to my side of the window and handed me a homemade pamphlet with the words "The Branch Davidians" on the front in darkened letters, followed by a series of scrawled words covering at least ten pages. "My daughter was murdered there," she pointed to the remains of the compound, her gnarled fingers were twisted as old oak roots often do in age.

"I'm so sorry," I told her, taking the pamphlet. I knew the draw of men like Koresh all too well. The appeal of magnetism and authority mixed with a kind of secret-knowledge-let-me-save-you-and-fuck-you charm was, at least for a girl entering her teenage years, hard to resist. How men gained such control over not only women but also a group of people was undeniable. How men could send someone to their grave simply by ordering them to do so. How this extended down into many Christian sects and private Christian schools. They groomed the young men by modeling a set of behaviors and the young women who learned their roles as submissives. I became part of this manipulation. She said nothing as we drove off, homeward bound, leaving the sadness of the site and the destruction behind us in the passenger-side mirror.

I didn't know what this meant at the time, but I came to understand this, Son. All too well. And in the end, I wasn't the same girl with the same hopes and dreams. Be careful what you set your intentions to. You just might get what you think you want.

Dear Lord, Save This Girl

Christian School of Colorado still stands on a hill overlooking Centennial Boulevard and the Pikes Peak mountain range. The principal back then, Mr. Corbett, was a tall, skinny man with dark hair cut close and wore the same small, round glasses. His mouth was set in a solid, thin, straight line every time I saw him, and the dress suits he wore fell too short in the arms and legs, which caused him to tug at them every few minutes. He was the epitome of every American 1950s era principal.

My first day of seventh grade felt like any kid's first day, filled with nerves and a little hope. I carried a small velvet jewelry bag I charged the night before with good intentions, filled with Yarrow and Angelica to help me be brave and make friends. Angela was already popular because everyone knew her older sister, Renee. I followed her around from classroom to classroom, feeling lost and vulnerable when we separated for different classes, watching her dark curls bounce against her back as she left me behind in the hallway. Students crowded around her, kids she already knew from gatherings at the school and other events with her sister. I was lost in a sea of students, nervous and wondering how I would manage to fit in. There weren't required uniforms, but everyone dressed modestly: Jeans, button-up shirts and blouses, tennis shoes. No cleavage. No midriffs. No foul language on clothing.

We bowed our heads and prayed before the teacher started the lesson in each class. I kept my head up, not knowing what to do. The other kids stared at me until I slowly lowered my head, watching them as they squeezed their eyes shut, lips moving in prayer. I didn't know how to pray, and I didn't know the memorized lines *Dear-Lordprotectusfromthisdayandofferusthestrengthtoacceptnewchallenges* being sing-sung as smooth as song lyrics. The overwhelming feeling of floating into a world of people and religion I was not familiar with felt isolating as crowds of kids pushed themselves through narrow hallways filled with aging beige carpet and lines of metal lockers. I searched for Angela as I headed to the lunchroom, trying to spot her dark curly hair and the bright pink shirt she finally decided on after days of agonizing over her first-day-of-school outfit. Before I could find her, I became aware of a herd of students stampeding toward me in the hallway. The group was walking quickly, hands balled into fists, lips pursed, eyes locked on me while everyone else in the hall cleared a path for them. I opened my mouth to protest and started to walk away, but they formed a circle around me, blocking any hope of escape. One of them, an older boy named Paul, held a thick, black bible in his hands. He opened it. The crisp pages against his fingers sounded like wood cracking. A million hands began to touch my face, arms, and back. I didn't know what was happening. Didn't know if this was some kind of initiation for new students. A junior high hazing. The other students in the hallway all stopped to watch, and the sound of buzzing began from somewhere close to me. It soon became clear it wasn't buzzing at all; it was their words, their rapid-fire prayers: *DearLordsavethisgirlfromhersinssheknowsnotwhat-shedoestoattractSatanbutwefeelhimandaskforyourprotectionagainsthissin Oh Lord Oh Lord Oh Lord!* hands were on me, beige carpet, on my hands and knees, still searching for Angela to save me. All I could see were legs and feet. Paul stood above me with his bible, smiling, his teeth perfect and white. Above him, the fluorescent hallway lights cast a faded yellow halo around his dark curls.

"Save this girl, Oh Lord, for she is ugly with sin and has brought Satan along with her!

My mind flashed back to Veronica, and even though we were only kids messing around, I wondered if Paul was right, if he could see something dark in me that no one else could. His hands touched my face, the top of my head, and there was a surge of electricity between us. He smiled down at me, and I stopped trying to move. The air between us became thick with silence. He slammed his bible shut and reached his free hand down to me, lifting me as much as the tight pulse of the crowd would allow. Still holding my hand, he faced me, performing for the in-between class rush in the hallway.

"Do you accept the Lord Jesus Christ as your Savior from this day forward?" His voice boomed as he brought me closer to him, his face intent. I could smell the scent of his soap—Ivory or Dial—and something else on his skin, something that made me shake. "Do you?" he whispered, squeezing my hand. I heard the buzz of the lights overhead, the shuffle of impatient shoes against the carpet, small chatter. At that moment, it was just the two of us. He's holding my hand and looking at me like no boy has before. Nodding his head, encouraging me, I found myself nodding along with him. He mouths the word "yes," and I hear myself say it too, *Yes, Yes, whatever he wants, just yes.* His hand was warm and soft against mine, and his breath on my face smelled like sweet mint toothpaste, and everyone was smiling at me as he raised our hands together in the air and declared, "She is saved! She is saved!" He dropped my hand, and I still felt his sweat in my palm, warm and slick, as I wiped it against my leg, already wanting more of him.

The day I was saved in the hallway of my junior high school, I chose to allow them to believe I had accepted Jesus Christ into my heart as my Lord and Savior, that their laying of hands upon me saved my soul. Some people think laying hands will cure illness and save someone from dying. But I only wanted Paul's hands on me. Paul was my only motivation for getting up in the morning from that day forward. He had me from that first day in the hallway, and from then on, it was my goal to make him notice me. This meant learning everything I could about the Bible and Christianity. This meant hiding my past with Veronica and the spells we had done. This meant turning into someone I wasn't.

"There is nothing covered that will not be revealed and hidden that will not be known." (Matthew 10:26).

Dream Fuck

Mom stood in the kitchen making coffee. Her dark blonde hair was sleep-tangled, and she looked exhausted. She'd been slumming the single mom life since the divorce, working full time in a cleanroom at Hewlett-Packard, wearing what she called a "Bunny Suit," a clean suit used to keep out any dirt or debris from contaminating the massive computers she worked around.

"You're going to hell," I told her with all of the righteousness of an Apostle.

"What the hell, Hillary?" Blue eyes wide, her mouth tight.

"Sorry, it's just, that's what they tell us at school. If you aren't saved, you go to hell." I shuffled my feet on the kitchen tile, feeling ashamed. I was still learning how to navigate the religion and the totality of accepting Jesus Christ as Lord and Savior as the golden ticket into Heaven. Without it, well, straight to hell you went.

"That's ridiculous. Don't let that school brainwash you, or I'm pulling you out. No daughter of mine is going to join some Christian Death Cult."

During my seventh-grade year, I learned to succumb to the beliefs of the school, its students, and its teachers to blend in and avoid trouble. I mirrored my outfits with what I saw the other girls wearing. Jeans, simple shirts, or sweaters, nothing that showed off anything that could be construed as "distracting." Jewelry was still worn but frowned upon. Students bejeweled their Bibles with stick-on beads, stickers, or ornate jewels. It seemed to be some kind of a competition on who could have the most blinged-out Bible. I noticed Angela blended herself in with the other girls in our class more and more, becoming bigger and brighter and more popular than she ever had been in elementary school. She slowly came to love the attention she got from everyone in our class and started hanging out with the Beckys and the Kristens, ditching me to figure out lunches and locker talks on my own. At the same time, I began to shrink myself, becoming camouflaged amongst the crowds of students in hallways, classrooms, and during breaks in between classes.

Every Tuesday during chapel, I sat in the back church pews, silently resenting everyone around me. It permeated off me like a stench. Chapel was the equivalent of a church service but mainly involved talking about issues students and faculty noticed for that week. As time went on, I became aware of how it was more of an opportunity to sing praise on someone or just the opposite, to call someone else's poor behavior out and shame them by saying they "weren't acting very Christ-like." A large section of the school's main building had been constructed to look like a church inside the school, complete with a pulpit and several stained-glass windows behind the main stage, which was used for church services, school assemblies, and plays. During chapel, I stole God's Time to write, using my Bible as a cover to write short stories and terrible poetry. I drew Tarot cards and hoped each time I would pull The Lovers as I stared at the back of Paul's head bowed in prayer, exposing the back of his neck. Paul was The King of Wands each time I pulled a card on him, a fire and energy that transcended the cards. The heat I felt for him engulfed me until I could feel my whole body burning. As I stared at the back of his bent neck, I wondered what it would be like to wrap my hands around him, feel his skin on mine. But I knew his interest in me stopped at saving me or trying to save me, in the biblical sense, not in the romantic, Hollywood movie, teen drama way that I wanted. Still, I continued to obsess over him, hoping one day he would look past the Jesus between us and see me.

Chapel was also when kids like Jeremiah Ruiz used the opportunity to belt out songs about The Lord and God and any other cliched tropey Christian themes that could be manipulated into words. It was the Christian version of *The Voice*, but the principal and teachers acted as judges, and the students were the audience. Jeremiah Ruiz was known for his perfect-pitched booming voice as he stood, legs apart atop the stage in front of the stained-glass windows, belting out songs about carrying burdens and finding Jesus. Every Tuesday, the school staff and faculty chose the Singer of the Week, and the student's picture was hung in a golden plastic frame on the wall by the trophy case. For three months straight, Jeremiah Ruiz had been Singer of the Week, and he wasn't about to lose his title.

"My cross is my burden to bear, Oh Lord, Oh Lord, Oh LOOOORRRRDDD!" The students all raised their hands in the air, slowly swaying back and forth as dreamy smiles spread across their faces, eyes squeezed shut in ecstasy as they waited for God to bless them. I felt I was living in a surreal world, where reality existed somewhere hidden, behind the school's brick walls or inside the complicated system of tunnels that led to the basement beneath, hidden behind the cranky old furnace puffing bursts of heat. It wasn't anything I could put my finger on specifically, but a series of incidents and attitudes, people, and beliefs that all built toward one conclusion in my early teenage mind: these people were the equivalent of a cult with the freedom of still trying to win popularity contests amongst each other. It was an ego contest to see who could out fake everyone else.

While the battle of the best voice continued, I wrote my darkest stories as a way to balance my brain, to save myself from losing my mind from a bombardment of raptured Bible verses taken out of context and blown up to fit whatever life struggle the song was meant to preach about. In my first year at CSC, I tried to fit in as best I could, but I still received threats from the Sports Girls, a group of seventh, eighth, and ninth graders on the famous CSC girls basketball team. Their frontrunner was a tall, square-jawed girl with small eyes and light curly hair named Tanya, who threatened to kick my ass because I "looked at her funny." The Sports Girls took up all of the space in the hallways and lunchroom as they palmed basketballs, soccer balls, or whatever balls they were playing with that season, staring people down as they gawked in fear and admiration. Their jock energy permeated whatever room they were in, filling it with all of their bad bravadoes. Tanya had started a rumor that I was practicing witchcraft and hexing her team to lose, which caused the team to target me in the hallways and during class when the teacher was preoccupied. They would throw balls of wadded-up paper at me and call my house, whispering in the phone, "I'm going to kick your ass," then quickly hung up. The witchcraft rumors weren't far from the truth. I was still practicing spells and reading Tarot, but it had nothing to do with them specifically. And I never confirmed the label they placed on me: I never called myself a witch. I kept school as separate from my life at home as I could, wanting the world I created in my room at my dad's apartment and my mom's house to be as far away from school life as possible. Besides, their threats were small and petty and still didn't stack up to what I would be facing with Veronica if I left to go to the public junior high.

By the time the spring snow stopped, and temperatures warmed into the upper 60s and 70s, signaling the beginning of summer, I was spending less time with Angela and most of my time with Corinne, a friend I met in third grade. We wrote stories in spiral notebooks with fancy pens stolen from her mom's study, sometimes hiding out in the basement's empty bathtub to avoid having to do chores and writing as the hours ticked by. Sometimes we walked down to the corner store and bought sweet and sour candy and fruit-flavored soda, exploring the back alleyways and dirt bike trails on our side of town, far from Angela's neighborhood. By the time eighth grade started, Corinne had gone to her junior high, and I returned to find Angela, one of the most popular girls in our grade and on her way to matching her older sister's legacy as "Voted Most Popular." I had become all but invisible save for a few friends who were lesser-knowns but cool as fuck. Macy, who was all about race car driving and ferrets, and Morgan, slightly nerdy and mousy and didn't talk shit like most of the other girls in our class. We threw down my Tarot cards at lunch away from prying eyes, giggling when The Devil card surfaced when we asked about the popular group, including Angela. I found solace in my two friends while watching my friendship with Angela slip away. I no longer spent the night at her house or went swimming at the Manitou Springs pool with her. We stopped hanging out in her huge backyard, where we had built altars and collected nature to display, all things her stepdad called "Satanic." By now, it was clear our friendship had changed.

Paul, who was in the ninth grade, had skyrocketed into Dream Fuck status and always had a group of students, both boys and girls, swarming around him at all times. Getting him alone was nearly impossible. The small efforts I did attempt, usually at the water fountain or between classes, purposely bumping into him or pretending to wait for someone next to him, went completely unnoticed. It never slid past me that he and Angela were hanging out more and more, though Angela had sworn to me at the beginning of summer she would never talk to Paul or pay any attention to him. When summer ended, and it had become clear we were no longer best friends, I watched as the inevitable gravitation of the popular girl towards Dream Fuck slowly began. But I couldn't stop myself from continuing to obsess over Paul or at least the idea of him and wasn't ready to drop him as my full-time fantasy. I kept to myself, hung out with Macy and Morgan, and avoided everyone in my class as best I could, which wasn't hard. I was invisible.

☿

My eighth-grade Bible Studies teacher, Mr. Garret, loved to hear himself talk. Every day, he would start the class by sharing a story he thought was relevant and *didactic* to teenagers.

"Do you know why it's important for everyone in this class to learn how to drive a stick shift?" he asked the class as he walked up and down the aisles. He did this to scan everyone's faces to ensure all eyes were on him. "Because once, not that long ago, I felt a great pain in my heart. Actual pain in my heart." He paused to clamp a fist to his chest. "And that night, we had a bible meeting group in our basement, and my wife had left to grab a pizza for everyone, taking the minivan." Mr. Garret stopped his meandering up and down the aisles and paused, frozen, before continuing his speech. "The minivan was an automatic, as you know, and the other vehicle we had, a 1980s Toyota Corolla, was not." Someone in the back of the

room made a noise of disgust at the mention of "Toyota Corolla."
Mr. Garret turned on his heel and pointed at the back of the room.

"Toyotas are fine vehicles, Mr. Myers. FINE!" Bryan Meyers scooted
further down in his seat as if Mr. Garret's finger willed him to do so,
his face reddening at the attention of being called out. Another turn
of his heel, and Mr. Garret was back to pacing.

"I had a pain in my heart, a stabbing pain, and I knew something
was wrong. Was it Satan? I called upon the name of Our Lord, and
he told me to tell my students." Heel, turn, a soldier in formation.
"But I didn't want to scare them. So, I said, does anyone here have
their driver's license? And you know that only one student raised her
hand. That student was Stephanie Freemason."

The students all began to clap, but Mr. Garret put his hand up,
immediately silencing the room. I had heard of Stephanie Freemason
and the rumors that Mr. Garret was having a sexual relationship with
her, but there was never any proof that surfaced. Still, I saw how
Mr. Garret favored her. Everyone did. A light brush with his hand
against her shoulder. Stares that lasted too long. Special Bible study
groups at his house in his basement, Mrs. Garret upstairs watching
her TV shows. So unsuspecting. The thought of his naked chest and
its overgrown dark curly hair that stuck out like pubic hairs from
the top of his shirts made me gag. Dropping his hand to his side,
he continued his march up and down the aisles, eventually stopping
next to me.

"Miss Freemason, despite having her driver's license, did not
know how to drive a stick shift. So—" he pounded his fist on the top
of my desk as I startled and jumped in my seat. He looked down at
me. "Wouldn't you know, we got in that old Toyota Corolla, and I
told her how to operate that stick shift, and she managed to get me
right to the hospital emergency room. And oh, Holy Spirit! I was

experiencing a heart attack, folks. And Miss Freemason saved my life."

I rolled my eyes, and he smiled down at me, pushing himself away from my desk as he walked toward the front of the classroom. "But I do believe," he shouted, turning his back to us to write something in giant letters on the whiteboard, "that divine intervention played as much a part of my survival as Miss Freemason driving me to the hospital did." He stepped away so we could all read the words DIVINE INTERVENTION on the whiteboard. He set the dry erase marker down and clapped his hands together.

"Divine intervention. The act of God to either stop something bad from occurring or cause something good to happen. But," a raise of his index finger in the air. "Only if you believe, folks. Because if you haven't accepted our Lord and Savior Jesus Christ into your heart, divine intervention won't save you. Nothing will. No one can save you but Jesus Christ."

He turned and wrote on the whiteboard underneath DIVINE INTERVENTION: "Many are the plans in the mind of a man, but it is the purpose of the Lord that will stand." (Proverbs 19:21)

He locked eyes with mine, and I knew he knew. I was a liar. A deceiver. I only claimed to be saved so that Paul would like me. I would never be one of them, and I would never be saved. Not in the way they believed I should, by Jesus, a man who sacrificed himself to the very men who would kill him.

At the time, I told myself I would never sacrifice myself for someone else. Time has a way of changing old beliefs. Old standoffs within yourself. I would find out years later just how wrong I was, Son.

Embodied Relationship With the Divine

Mrs. White taught 8th grade English and was the wife of Mr. White, the history teacher. A month prior, Mr. White had given me an F on my report on Charles Manson and the book *Helter Skelter*. At the time, I was going through my obsession with serial killers and cults, and *Helter Skelter* was the perfect combination of both. I showed my dad the assignment requirements and my report and watched as his face turned red with anger. "He gave you an F because you did a report on a cult leader instead of on a safer subject," he told me. I knew exactly what I was doing and wasn't going to back down, but I also didn't care about the failing grade. My dad did. After a confrontation in person, Mr. White changed my grade from an F to a B-, claiming my sources weren't cited accordingly. I didn't challenge him, knowing I'd won the battle.

Mrs. White was your typical meek Christian wife: soft-spoken, small, and forgettable unless challenged, in which case she forgot who and where she was. It wasn't often, but when it did happen, she used her voice to command the attention of God. I found myself torn between despising her and admiring her. In the middle of explaining conjunctions and how to use them in sentences, she turned to face the whiteboard when a bright red stain began to spread across the back of her white linen skirt. The classroom filled with soft laughter, becoming louder and louder. Mrs. White turned around and faced the class, face as red as the stain on her skirt, ready to command the classroom to silence, when she looked down and saw the blood blooming on her skirt. Her entire demeanor changed from confrontational back to meek to less than meek, and she ran out of the room crying. The entire classroom erupted in howls of laughter from the boys, but the girls all sat in silence as we met each other's eyes, a silent kind of horror filling the room with the weight of our knowing.

"The pilgrims see Mary Magdalene as the guardian of menstrual blood and advocate a 'feminist reading' of Jesus' message. They perform creative rituals to commune with 'Mother Earth' by offering Her their menstrual blood…The pilgrims' rituals of offering also foster an embodied relationship with the divine[i]."

---

[i] Journal of Ritual Studies © 2014 Pamela J. Stewart and Andrew J. Strathern

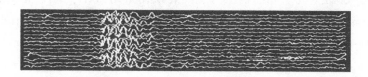

A field could be seen behind my school building in the first grade, stretching for miles until it ended abruptly at the foothills. Part of the field belonged to a man named Mr. Olinger and was guarded by his dog named Kodiak. Cutting through Kodiak's field was a rite of passage for many fifth graders going into sixth grade at my school. A pre-teen hazing. I heard the third graders talking about Kodiak how he attacked kids. The owner refused to tie him up or keep him inside. Kodiak was a Siberian Husky, all white, with gray on the tip of his tail and ears. His eyes were red like Lite Brite pegs, and he was known to eat rabbits he killed during the day. The blood from his prey stained his coat from white to dark burgundy. His owner didn't need to feed him. Kodiak was a natural killer.

I pushed through the wall of weeds and jumped the chain-link fence into the open field. The milkweed rubbed against my bare legs as I kept my eyes out for anything white and fluffy as I made my way through the tall stalks of sunflowers and bees that floated above the blooms. I made it halfway through the field and was still deep in thought when I heard the noise. It sounded like a blender starting up at first; slow, on what my mom called *mince mode,* then became louder and faster, until I realized the noise was growling. I turned to look behind me, seeing only rows and rows of sunflowers as they bowed their heads in submission to the wind. I could see the fence and the other side of the field where my house was. During that year, I read a copy of the *Encyclopedia Britannica* at school for our weekly project on wild animals. The segment warned to never, ever run away from an animal stalking you. You'll only draw attention to yourself. My teacher told my class it's the same as painting yourself bright red and running through a field of white flowers. *Animals see colors we don't. And some see in the darkness.* I knew then, as I later came to know as an adult in a relationship with a monster, to never, ever draw attention to myself.

I didn't run, but I started to walk faster, my skirt hem catching on all the sharp, pointed thistles and pulling them out as I brushed past them. I kept my face forward, my eyes on the end of the field, and I felt my heart pounding in my throat. The blender noise started up again somewhere behind me, but this time it was closer, and it wasn't minced mode anymore. This time it was what my brother called *mangle.*

"Mom's mangling something in the blender again," He would laugh. "Remember that scene in *Gremlins?* That's what Mom's doing to dinner right now." I didn't want to be mangled or minced, and despite what the *Encyclopedia Britannica* told me, I started to run. The mangling noise turned into vicious barking behind me, but I didn't look back. I could see the fence, and behind the fence, the sidewalk leading to home. I knew I was close. I knew Kodiak was close, too. With the growling at my back and just a few feet remaining, I squeezed my eyes shut and sprinted for the fence, the world spread out in front of me, wide open.

A Spell to Find Someone Out

Use a white porcelain bowl and fill with water. Use 7 toothpicks and place them on the surface of the water with your right hand. Cover with a white towel and raise one end. Whisper into the bowl:

"Tell me what I wish to see."

Blow three times on the water, then leave the bowl under your bed. In the morning, the toothpicks will have formed the initials of the person causing you trouble.

Sometimes you only see what you want to see.

The Devil's Work

The purpose of the Genesis story is to explain the loss of that long, slow paradise that today we call the Paleolithic—an epoch of history in which our ancestors lived not only in a sustainable relationship to the Earth but in a joyous and loving one as well. In one of the greatest bait and switches of all time, that loss is blamed on Eve, whose name means, tellingly, "Mother of All Life[ii]."

When it was time for the Fall Social, I had begun amping my efforts to get Paul to notice me in the hopes he would say yes to being my date. I was slowly coming into my own during this time and started wearing tight clothing to show off more of my body—a body I was still getting used to—a body that would later endure so much pain and pleasure I would be confused as to what its purpose was for years to come. What I did know was bodies had power, and

---

[ii] *The Way of the Rose: The Radical Path of the Divine Feminne Hidden in The Rosary,* Clark Strand and Perdita Finn

I could use that power to get what I wanted instead of succumbing to what others wanted.

I began to drift back to my books from the library, many of which I found at the local bookstore. Once I was able to own them, I discovered more and more resources becoming available on spellcraft and traditions than when I was in elementary school, which was a new and special kind of excitement for me. I found myself in an unusual position of studying, memorizing, and reciting both the Bible and what I was learning from the many witchcraft and folk magic books I was discovering in the library. Someone was ordering the books, and this seemed impossible in a town filled with Christianity and military bases. I wondered who and who I could talk to and share what I was learning. Still, I persisted in my studies, reading and absorbing everything I could, both in the biblical texts as well as the areas of magick and craft, realizing there was a connection between the two that was always passed off as "witchcraft" or "The Devil's Work" whenever it was brought up in Bible class. Knowing now, it has more to do with eclecticism and what I was most interested in— the women of the Bible. How Lilith was vilified as a demon for refusing to lie beneath Adam, yet the truth behind the scriptures and the real interpretation of Lilith was always avoided. How the interpretations of Mary were twisted to sustain the misogynistic beliefs of the men in power, and how even the school and its major financial supporter, Focus on the Family, made Mary out to be someone she was not. Submissive. Virginal. Never separated from the men she was surrounded by, both in scripture and her life. Mary and Lilith became my figureheads—two women persecuted and falsified throughout time. I sought out as much information as I could find on the truth behind both of them. I read about Catholicism and how Marian Apparitions—a supernatural appearance by Mary—still had to be approved by a man, the pope, to be considered believable.

Despite her appearance and her need to communicate a message to both men and women over centuries, there still had to be a process in place, enforced by a man, to be deemed authentic. My teachers continued to lecture us on how women should be subservient to men or risk becoming a symbol of evil. But I knew the sections I was reading in other areas of the Bible that weren't being taught in class were being twisted into what they wanted us to believe. I read everything I could on Lilith and The Witch of Endor—any female figure marked as a demon or sorceress in biblical terms—to come to my own conclusions. Everything they were teaching us was manipulation, so I began to read the sections they weren't assigning us to read in Bible class, both new and old testament, to try to learn on my own what was the truth.

"So Moses and Aaron went to Pharaoh and did just as the Lord commanded. Aaron threw his staff down in front of Pharaoh and his officials, and it became a snake. Pharaoh then summoned wise men and sorcerers, and the Egyptian magicians also did the same things by their secret arts: Each one threw down his staff, and it became a snake. But Aaron's staff swallowed up their staffs" (Exodus 7:11)

I knew there was power in my body and what I was learning, in what I possessed and was still becoming. Either I could control it, or it would be controlled by others. But as a fourteen-year-old girl still not sure what it was to be a woman, I didn't know the dangers of what a woman's body meant in a man's world—in the gaze of so many men in positions of power. How unrealistic and unkind the expectations of Hollywood and magazines are to a real woman's body. How those expectations of sex and body image fuck with girls and women and their own exploration of pleasure. Still, I was a teenager, and I wanted Paul in a way I didn't understand yet. I knew from overhearing the boys during gym class talk about jerking themselves off to whichever actress or model was popular at the time that even though the subject was taboo, and even though the school touched on the subject of masturbation as a sin, they didn't outright punish those who talked about it. So, the boys talked about it endlessly while the girls giggled as if they weren't doing the same (or maybe repressing it), as if it was shameful if we did talk about pleasuring ourselves. How even the Turner Twins—Ruth and Mary—once told someone in our class in confidence that when they were younger, they had "explored each other's naked bodies" and were mortified when the secret got out. As if our bodies weren't worth learning about in the most intimate of ways—ways that we as women should understand long before a lover ever touches us.

At night, under my sheets, I touched myself and thought about Paul touching me, what he would do to me if we ever had a chance to be alone together. But as the fantasy continued on, night after night, it turned from Paul touching me to focusing on how my body responded to my own touch—what got me off by my own hands. What's now more widely known as using sex within magick, or "sex magick," though I didn't have a name for it back then, became a forefront of my own observations. What started out as imagining Paul's face in my moment of climax became visualizing myself busting out through the doors of the school with all of the confidence of someone I previously thought I could never become, leaving the school behind me forever. I hoped I would never lose this ability to connect my body with the energy and power I felt within me before any man had ever laid hands on me. My body was my body, and I had total control of it. If only this remained true into adulthood. But things we are passionate about in childhood have a way of undoing themselves so quickly, so mindlessly. How easy it is for us to make exceptions to boundaries when it comes in the name of love.

Don't Set Your Expectations Too High, Honey

When The Fall Social was officially announced, everyone began talking about who they were going with, what they were going to wear, and who had already been asked to go. I knew it was time to ask Paul to go with me. Between passing periods, I found him at his locker, alone—at least momentarily—and my window of opportunity was closing. I took a deep breath and walked up to him, my entire body sweating. I stood and watched the side of his face as he pulled books out of his locker, noticing how he had a scattering of freckles across the bridge of his nose I hadn't seen before. He turned and caught me staring at him, his eyes flickering with surprise.

"Oh, hi."

"Hi, Paul." Awkward silence. He held his books in front of us like a shield.

"Um, so, I was wondering, are you going to the Fall Social?" I wanted to die already. I wanted the carpet to rip open beneath my feet and swallow me.

"Yeah, so, I am. I'm going with Angela."

My heart sank. It did more than sink. It dropped into my gut with all of the weight of my entire universe. I couldn't say anything, my face was burning hot, and I couldn't let him continue to stare at me like he was. I wanted The Rapture to happen at that exact moment, for the roof of the building to rip open while the trumpets blared and Heaven itself opened up and sucked me into a giant pink cloud.

Paul stared at me, and the roof didn't peel off by The Hand of God, so I turned and ran as fast as I could, down the hall, out the front doors, and into the parking lot. I sat on the curb until passing period was over, staring up into the sky and damning God under my breath. Damning Paul, damning Angela. The betrayal I felt, knowing that Angela knew how much I secretly liked Paul based on one of our last conversations as friends we had together. Knowing how I confided in Angela, how her dark eyes grew bigger and bigger as I told her like I was sharing a secret meant for Hollywood itself, now felt like a sick, heavy weight inside of me.

Months went by, and I was so full of rage the only outlet I found was writing stories inside my secret notebooks during class, wishing one day I could get them published and get the fuck out of Colorado Springs. I still have all of those notebooks, all of the stories. It's a reminder of my mindset. My passion for writing. Sometimes, that girl doesn't seem that far away despite the years. My dad supported my interest in writing and took me to The Broadmoor Hotel one night for a special author's event. My dad and I sat side by side on padded chairs as a man stood on a stage, his book propped up next to him on a display table, with a giant photo blown up behind him on a white screen of a man bundled up in a blanket lying on a park bench covered in snow.

"And I knew when I snorted those ten lines of coke it was the end of my marriage," Dramatic pause, the microphone in his hand slowly being squeezed. "the end of my career, and the end of the life I knew as a top financial advisor, a father, and a husband. I knew I had lost everything and succumbed to the temptation and sins of drugs, sex, and, well, not rock and roll, but you know what I mean." I side-eyed my dad and sighed, wondering if this was how all authors spoke at their author events. How all books were marketed and published and found audiences. If so, I wanted nothing to do with the publishing world. I couldn't imagine the books I was reading— poetry, fantasy, horror— could ever be as ridiculous as the writer standing on stage in front of me. He made a mockery of the sacred act of writing, and I wanted nothing to do with it.

After his speech, my dad made me wait for him to sign a copy of his book, titled something along the lines of "How Courage and Love Conquer All." My dad handed the man a pre-purchased book, and he took it, starting up at me expectantly, his face sweating from his hour-long speech. "Oh, sign it to Hillary, two L's," my dad told him. He scribbled something with a black Sharpie and snapped the book shut, handing it to my dad.

"My daughter here is an aspiring writer," My dad said, and I felt myself turn bright red with the heat of utter mortification. I tugged on his arm, but he ignored me, thinking he was doing his best by attempting to connect me with this man. The writer raised his dark eyebrows at me, his face pockmarked and greasy. "Really?" He looked me up and down, sizing me up, already judging me in his mind, framing me in the light of Author, and seeing if I fit. I am a dead tree swaying in the overhead ceiling fan's breeze. Something so special and secret to me, the act of writing itself without the label of "writer" was now being pushed on me without my consent, and this man who knew nothing about me was measuring me based on his own experiences, which were not mine, would never be mine. He and I were as different as night and day.

"She is. Any advice you can give her?"

"Yeah, don't set your expectations too high, honey," he snorted, reaching his hand out for the next book to be signed by the next adoring fan, dismissing us. My dad and I walked away silently, both embarrassed for different reasons.

"Dad, I—." But before I could tell him I appreciated him supporting me, how I believed that bringing me to the reading was his way of being supportive despite the guy being a total douchebag, he dropped the book into one of the trash cans lining the hallway. The weight of the words landed with a thud on top of discarded soda cans and half-eaten food items leftover from the refreshment table. I smiled as we walked out to the parking lot and didn't say anything. We didn't have to. Years later, my dad would give me a Moleskine notebook after my first short story was published, telling me, "I'm told this is what writers all use." I never used the notebook. I still have it on my bookshelf, untouched, too scared to ruin its sacredness, but the gesture of my dad gifting me that Moleskine meant more to me than he'll probably ever know.

I knew I would be an author and write whatever I wanted one day. Men like Mr. Garret singled the weak out and humiliated them. About boys like Paul, who used the same magnifying cult-leader manipulations on me that continued to draw me in as the months passed by. He and Angela were The Dream Fuck Couple after The Fall Social, yet he continued to stare at me in the hallways, brushing his body against mine when passing me by, watching me drink from the water fountain by the bathrooms. At first, I didn't understand it. Why he acted like he was interested in me if he was with Angela.

My confusion soon faded into reciprocation, and I began to tease him, wiping the dripping water from my lips with the back of my hand slowly while meeting his eyes if I was at the water fountain or locking eyes with him if he was sitting in the lunchroom across from my table. I didn't know exactly what I wanted from him, but I sensed what he wanted from me, and it scared me and made me feel alive in a way I had never felt before. Maybe he was with Angela, but it was clear that he wanted me, or was messing with me, whatever that meant. My own special junior high version of David Koresh. I knew there was power in sexuality, and I used my newly found sex magick whenever I could. Still, had Paul and I ever found ourselves alone together, I would probably run and hide. I might have found my power in my own body, but I was still too naive to know how to use that power and sexuality with someone else.

Thou Shalt Not Suffer a Witch to Live

"The Rapture," Mr. Garret told us in Bible class one day, his finger pointed in the air as if signaling the very end, "will come, no doubt about that." His eyes darted around, looking sharply at unsuspecting students. "But will you be wearing all that jewelry you love to wear, Miss Anderson? Those fancy sports watches, Mr. Williams? Because when the rapture hits, all that will be left, for those called into Heaven to be with Our Lord and Savior Jesus Christ, will be a pile of jewelry." He stopped at my desk, avoiding making eye contact, something I had become accustomed to over the years. We both knew his presence was enough. We didn't need to meet eyes. "And that's why I want you to play Satan in the upcoming play." He tapped my hand with his fingers.

"Excuse me?" I asked, pulling my hand away from under his.

"You heard me. I think you would make a wonderful Satan. What with your natural ability to scare people." The whole class laughed, encouraging him to continue. "I mean, just look at you, what, with all your black clothes. Don't think for a minute I don't see that Tarot deck you keep in your bag either. Have you talked to your Christ Advisor? I don't believe this school or this entire entity accommodates witchcraft, do you?" I shook my head, face burning, staring at the cracks in my desk, wondering how long it took for the wood to succumb to each body that sat in its confines over the years, how many bodies had sat in my place before me, feeling humiliated and singled out every day, as I had.

"So, what do you think, class? Do we say *Yay* or *Nay?*"

A resounding *yay!*

☿

In the final months of ninth grade, I had already made plans to register at the local high school, the same school Corinne was going to. My mom thought Corinne was a bad influence, but the joke was on her—the reality was that I was the bad influence. I was the one who kept pushing the envelope with Corinne, who became my agreeable sidekick, the two of us slowly fulfilling our roles as Thelma and Louise, minus the suicide pact. We had big plans to finish high school together, attend the same college, become famous writers, and live a life of travel and no responsibilities. I had survived three years at CSC. Going to my neighborhood high school was the only freedom I felt and wanted. As seventh, eighth, and ninth grade came and passed, Angela and I no longer spoke, and Paul slowly became less of an obsession. As a teenager, I understood that most beliefs the school and the teachers instilled were created on misinterpretations and falsehoods. I couldn't understand why adults choose to place their blind faith in a school and religion that only served their own best interests—never anyone else's. By the time I left CSC, I became saturated with a special kind of teenage rage that could have only manifested from three years of being forced to be someone you weren't. Everything surrounding you is based on The Rapture and the idea that all of our sins would be washed away when the end came, a guaranteed golden ticket into Heaven. But the end wasn't coming, at least not in the way they believed it was.

On the final day of ninth grade, while the halls were empty and everyone had already cleaned out all of their lockers, I walked through the hallways, finally feeling like I could walk in the middle, not on either side, not making myself as small as possible. I stretched out my arms and started to run, screaming and shouting nonsense, laughing, as I kicked open the No Exit doors leading to the back entry and parking lot where the city bus would come and take me home. As I got on the bus and found my usual seat in the back, I watched out the window as we pulled away from the school for the last time. The giant white cross disappeared over the hill of Austin Bluffs Parkway, and I knew I would never have to stare up at that cross again as I entered the school's walls. The giant Lion's picture with the words CSC in gold letters on the front of my school binder offered me no comfort. A lion will only protect its own if threatened by another male lion or predator. I never wanted to be a lion.

I closed my eyes as the bus slowly rocked its way down the road. I imagined striking a single match and throwing it at Mr. Garret's face, Paul's face, Angela's face, everyone's face, then lighting more matches, more matches, until the entire book was empty and I was surrounded by flames, watching as the school around me burned to the ground until there was nothing left but a pile of ash.

"Thou shalt not suffer a witch to live" (Exodus 22:18).

Government Dependent Whore

You once asked me if we could order a Dad[iii] off the internet. You pointed to the computer screen at an image of a man. He was wearing casual clothes and smiling at something in the distance. I

[iii] Dads, for instance, love their children "more dangerously." That's because they play "rougher" and are more likely to encourage risk-taking. They provide kids with a broader diversity of social experiences. They also introduce them to a wider variety of methods of dealing with life. They tend to stress rules, justice, fairness, and duty in discipline. In this way, they teach children the objectivity and consequences of right and wrong. They give kids insight into the world of men. They prepare them for the challenges of life and demonstrate by example the meaning of respect between the sexes. In connection with this last point, research indicates that a married father is substantially less likely to abuse his wife or children than men in any other category.

Fathers encourage competition, engendering independence. Mothers promote equity, creating a sense of security. Dads emphasize conceptual communication, which helps kids expand their vocabulary and intellectual capacities. Moms major in sympathy, care, and help, thus demonstrating the importance of relationships. Dads tend to see their child in relation to the rest of the world. Moms tend to see the rest of the world in relation to their child. Neither style of parenting is adequate in and of itself. Taken together, they balance each other out and equip the up-and-coming generation with a healthy, well-rounded approach to life.

https://www.focusonthefamily.com/family-qa/the-significance-of-a-fathers-influence/

laughed, but it wasn't funny. I told you a Dad can't be ordered off the internet, even though you can order a pizza or a wife. You were always searching for a man to show you how to be a man. You didn't need a dad, and I didn't need a man to be that dad to you, but I was wrong.

Being a single mother isn't what society or the movies make it out to be. Even the phrase itself: *I'm a single mother,* instantly labels me as divorced, government handout, food stamps, child support dependent, sugar daddy-seeker. A Government Dependent Whore. For me, there is no co-parenting. No weekend custody, parenting plans, or who gets whom during which holiday. A solo[iv] mother is entirely alone, left to her own devices to raise a child.

Finding a job that allows a single parent to work and take care of their child was next to impossible. It was always a matter of one or the other. A scramble to find a consistent daycare that was affordable. I couldn't turn down a job, so I wound up paying up to $1,000 a month at one point for full-time daycare. I had no help and no one nearby to watch you or even pick you up or drop you off. I found myself relenting to the needs of any company I worked for, never mentioning that I had a child during an interview in case it was cause for concern to not hire me. Likewise, once I was in a job position, I never called in sick if I needed to use those days for reasons I couldn't disclose, in case it was used against me later on. Pediatrician visits, dentist appointments, child sick days. Everything felt like a cover-up. I was always on edge, wondering when I would be written up if the

---

[iv] Despite the fact that cohabiting parents are younger and less educated than solo parents, they are still far less likely to be poor. All told, 16% of unmarried parents living with a partner are living below the poverty line, while about one-fourth (27%) of solo parents are. In comparison, just 8% of married parents are living in poverty.[7] Among solo parents, mothers are almost twice as likely as fathers to be living below the poverty line (30% vs. 17%), but poverty rates for cohabiting parents don't differ among mothers and fathers.
  https://www.pewresearch.org/social-trends/2018/04/25/the-changing-profile-of-unmarried-parents/04-24-18_singleparents-07/

daycare closed early due to weather or the thousands of other reasons a parent has to miss work.

I learned to hustle, to become resourceful. I got my game on. It wasn't always the best game, but I knew the rules and how to play it. If I had anything of value, I pawned it. If there was a paid market research study on consumer goods and services and I qualified, I did it. I'm an expert on bottled water and dishwasher detergent. I know what the target audience is. I know most commercials market toward middle-class, white, suburban couples. I know I do not belong to the target audience. I know it is better not to be in a target audience because you become a target.

My son, you have a monster for a father, and all you ever needed was a good person to show you how to be. Sometimes what we are missing is exactly what makes us stronger.

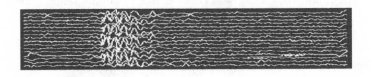

In the wild, male Orca will help raise offspring that are not their own. This is called *cooperative social structure*. They mate with numerous females and help raise their young, never committing to one female. This ensures the overall survival of a pod. This ensures all females and their calves are protected. Orca will train their young to hunt, often using prey as training tools, leaving the young calves to their own devices. It's not uncommon for an Orca to track a whale and her calf for days until finally, when the mother whale is too exhausted to defend herself, the Orca will move in, killing and eating the calf while the mother sends desperate distress signals, a scream for help.

I know that scream well, Son. But in our world, my screams are lost signals, searching for someone to hear us.

Pennyroyal Tea

After CCS, I attended my neighborhood public high school, Doherty, with Corinne, far away from Veronica and Angela and CCS. Corinne's mom was a southern Baptist who sold real estate and could often be found frying Spam in high heels and a skirt with a cigarette hanging out of her mouth. Corinne's stepdad later dedicated his life caring for her mom after she's diagnosed with Multiple Sclerosis and becomes bed-bound–watching daytime talk shows and soap operas, the smell of cigarette smoke and coffee permeating the rest of the house like a stain. I would sit on the edge of her bed and describe my day at school, telling her things I couldn't disclose to my own mother at the time, news about boys, and my fears of failure in school. She would nod and puff on her cigarette, always quick to soothe me with a gentle pat on my hand and a southern, "Well, honey, this is just a small part of a bigger life. Remember that." The image of her tall, thin figure and brown, curly hair, her southern drawl, and Elizabeth Taylor perfume—White Diamonds—would haunt me for years after. She became a second mother for as long as Corinne and I were friends.

Corinne and I spent our high school days drinking and hanging out with the skater and "freak" crowds—breaking into churches and burning bibles, drinking in empty Skate City parking lots, smoking weed, dropping acid, experimenting with everything society labeled as "bad," and smoking cigarettes, which later turned into an almost lifetime habit. I usually wound up holding Corinne's long, mermaidesque, wavy blonde hair away from her face as she threw up the night's alcohol because that's just what best friends did for each other. I chopped my hair short in a '20s style bob and dyed it midnight black, wore combat boots, and listened to L7, Bikini Kill, Nirvana, Sepultura, Salt-N-Pepper, Snoop Dogg, Beastie Boys, Ice Cube, Ministry, Danzig, and anything else that resonated the rage my generation was seething in. The young women we were meshed in with the young men in our class with almost no distinction. We were all caught up in a mid-90s generation that was born out of fusions of punk and metal music, Operation Desert Storm, the riots following the Rodney King trial, the bombing of The World Trade Center, and the rapper Biz Markie being sued for infringement, challenging sampling but also leading to a huge impact in popularity for hip hop in the suburbs of every small and big city in America, including my own. Los Angeles was on fire. We all watched on the TV as scenes played out in front of us in real-time. I could smell the smoke from the destruction as if it was leaking from the screen. Felt the pain and anger as palpable. I wrote bad poetry about boys I had crushes on and wrote decent short stories about love, death, and the usual dark themes that occupy a teenager's life in the middle of trying to figure shit out. Had you asked me back then the one thing I was pretty good at and had a passion for, it would always be writing. It was more a part of my being than an extension of myself even then.

My first boyfriend, Seth, was a disgruntled, typical bad boy skateboarder who was the spitting image of Kurt Cobain, but with bright purple-red hair, he often soaked in Tropical Punch Kool-Aid mix and vodka. I fell hard, losing my virginity to him within my first year of high school while the song "Detachable Penis" by King Missile played, and by the end, I found myself breaking up, then running back to him again and again. Any kind of power I wanted to wield over him was lost. He had total control over me, and he knew it. I couldn't get enough of him, and I did everything I could to spend as much time as possible with him—searching in the hallways at school or the back alleyways of the local pool halls.

"I will kick your stomach in if you wind up pregnant," he once told me, and I never doubted him. The sixteen-year-old me was terrified of him but couldn't stop myself from being obsessed. I was a pathetic, weak version of the woman I was in the process of becoming had I not fallen for this man who obviously had severe issues of his own that I wouldn't discover until after his suicide decades later. But back then, there were nights I would sneak out of my house, drive across town, and tap on his basement bedroom window to crawl into bed with him, his room smelling of incense and weed and cigarette smoke. His parents were divorced, and his dad let him be, for the most part, not caring what he did or with who. One night, after I had already crawled through his basement window, I discovered him drunk, waving a handgun around in the air. It was too late to turn back, and he wanted to pick a fight with me. Between his alcoholic-induced rage and me trying to escape up the basement stairs, he fired the gun, the bullet lodging itself in his bedside table. I ran but returned the next night again. Had I become pregnant with his baby, I wouldn't have known what to do, get an abortion, or struggle to raise a child on my own as a teenager. Living in the Christian-dominated town of Colorado Springs, with the heavy presence of Focus on the Family and its followers surrounding our high school, was confining and confusing. Often, devotees from Focus on the Family would show up in large groups outside of my high school with giant posters of aborted fetuses to terrify young teenagers into keeping unexpected pregnancies. These shock-value tactics neither hindered me from the thought of getting an abortion nor did they make me want to consider keeping a baby.

Rub a fresh egg counterclockwise over the womb beneath the naval. Recite The Lord's Prayer. Blow on the egg, then drop it slowly in a clear glass of water. If it sinks to the bottom, you are heavy with child. If it floats, you are not pregnant. If it floats then sinks, you will become pregnant within six months.

In 1993, Nirvana released their final studio album, *In Utero*, with a song called "Pennyroyal Tea," which, if anyone has heard or read the song lyrics, is about inducing a miscarriage. Seth sang this song to me constantly, balancing on his skateboard as he did so, laughing when he saw the look on my face.

Up until the 1800s, nearly every abortion was an herbal abortion. It wasn't until the 1970s that surgical abortion began to increase in popularity and safety after Roe v Wade. Prior to, abortifacient herbs were as strong an option as any other when considering abortion. In the right quantity, abortifacients can cause the uterus to contract and miscarry during pregnancy. They are often used in conjunction with 'helping herbs' or emmenagogue herbs like mugwort, rue, and blue cohosh, which stimulate blood flow to the uterus and promote menstruation.[v]

I think about Seth and how different my life would have been had I never managed to untangle myself from him. Maybe he wouldn't

_____

[v] Drink Me and Abort Your Baby: The Herbal Abortion Tea, Maya Lewis, Cuny Graduate School of Journalism. 12-16-2016

have put a bullet in his brain fifteen years later. Maybe he would have loved me the way I wanted him to love me. But I know none of this could be the reality I wanted for myself back then. And I don't know which was worse, the fact that I loved a boy who would never love me the way I needed to learn how to love in a healthy way or the fact that the 16-year-old part of me will always be in love with him to this day. How danger is confused with love and devotion. That sick, surreal, twisted teenage love that distorts our world when we are young and questioning everything and everyone. Years later, I saw Seth at a bowling alley in the Springs. He looked, well, happy. Or at least content. But he wasn't. He was on a trajectory straight towards a bullet, and no one knew. Years later, I drove down to The Springs and past Seth's old house, the one I spent so much time at during my teenage years. The window I would crawl through into his basement. I thought I would feel sadness and anger, white-hot, juicy rage, but I didn't. I felt relief.

Angela fell off my radar as friends often do when change happens and growing apart is inevitable. She lived a life of comfort and money, never having to struggle, always having a safety net underneath her to catch her whenever she fell. I resented her for it, for not wanting to seek out her own boundaries and to test herself and her resolve, but some people never dare to push themselves beyond their life of comfort. Never try to escape their confines. Her life of comfort still might have been hell for her in ways I could never know, and I can't fault her for something she had no control over. Remembering her now, the differences between her and I and the lives we led were as vast as the prairie grasslands that separate the Rocky Mountains from the eastern plains.

Their Cheatin' Hearts (Will Make You Weep)

Childhood plans never play out the way we dream they will, and neither did my friendship with Corinne or our post-high school plans. I moved to Durango, Colorado, for college and failed my first semester after succumbing to the typical temptations of drugs, alcohol, and too much freedom. I returned home to Colorado Springs to live, tail between my legs, and attended community college. College was a lot of responsibility, and I was too immature to handle the freedom handed to me after graduating high school months earlier. Corinne moved to Texas with her much older boyfriend and had to drop out of Texas A&M after six months when she became pregnant. Our friendship ended after she found Christ and pushed her God agenda on me. Too much trauma from the years I spent at CSC stayed with me, and the fact that the darker side of Christianity had gotten to my best friend was enough for me to turn my back on her and her beliefs. Still, I mourn the loss of our friendship like any physical death. The grief of losing her formed its own ghost inside of me, haunting me for years. Even now, I'll look her up on social media, look her mom up on Google to make sure she's still alive, seeing them both playing out their lives in smalltown Kansas. Just knowing they're still there gives me comfort. Nothing has changed. Sometimes that's better than death, even if it doesn't signal reconciliation.

I moved back in with my mom and stepdad, who were happy to let me live with them as long as I held a steady job and took classes. I worked as a cocktail waitress and maid cleaning houses, businesses, and motels. I saw the seedier side of humanity during this time, especially when it came to sex, whether in someone's private bedroom or in a pay-by-hour motel room. This is how I learned about sex toys and domination, escort services, and the men who used them. The women had no other choice but to use their bodies to make money. Often, while cleaning the motel rooms, I'd find the leftover remnants of an escort's evening. I became familiar with the clientele and the older men who hired them—a mix of middle-aged businessmen and lonely husbands looking for something that couldn't be filled with wives or booze or money. The woman who trained me, a trans woman named Candy, would often tell me stories about what she'd seen during her years working in hotels and motels across the country. She'd moved to Colorado Springs years earlier with two other friends who were transitioning as well, finding safety and comfort with each other in a small house they rented in Manitou Springs. Candy trained me to properly make a bed, safely handle sheets soaked in bodily fluids, and dispose of used, discarded sex toys.

"These men and their cheatin hearts," she sang to me in her best rendition of Patsy Cline, "will make you weep," a sad, sagging dildo in one hand and a pillow in the other. I admired Candy in a way that most of my friends in high school could never live up to. She taught me how to be safe in a world of sex and violence, where men were predators. More often than not, I watched her call the cops on men and their escorts, girls who didn't know any better who were being beaten inside their motel rooms. Her six-foot-tall, thin frame and hot roller curled platinum hair meant she never faded into the scenery. Candy was our protector and our mentor, a force within the confines of paper-thin walls and smoke-filled rooms.

It was while working graveyard hours as a cocktail waitress, without Candy there to look out for me, where many of my run-ins with men proved to be a threat. Men, I knew, when drinking a lot of alcohol and trying to numb their pain, would often hit on me and grab me, pulling me into their laps and forcing themselves on me. Once, a guy named Giovanni yanked me towards him on New Year's Eve and forced his lips on mine until the bartender, Dave, pushed him off of me. A fight ensued, and I ran, terrified, to the payphone inside the hallway to call my mom to please come get me. She showed up twenty minutes later still wearing her baby blue pajama bottoms and a pair of snow boots, the car's heater blasting. I tucked myself into the seat and buckled my seatbelt, my face forward, too humiliated to meet her eyes.

"I told you that job is dangerous," she put the car in reverse and headed out of the bar's parking lot toward home, the streets dark and covered in snow, the sound of the tires against ice filling the silence in the car. I didn't quit because I needed the money, and the tips were good, but I conceded that she was right. Of course, she was. She'd been a woman in this world longer than I had. Any woman knows when you put yourself in a situation where men can use any excuse to do whatever they want, you're constantly subjecting yourself to danger.

"Welcome to being a working woman in the world."

Especially the Hard Words

Writing about my different jobs was a way of remembering my experiences and processing them. I kept these writings to myself, never thinking they could be published one day, until a woman at the bar I was working at asked me what I was writing about, peering at me from behind her rocks glass as I scribbled words down in my flimsy spiral notebook with the bar pen. She wore her ash brown hair in lazy curls, thick-rimmed glasses, a lace top, and dress pants. She chain-smoked while grading papers at the bar most nights, and I was curious about what she did for work.

"You know, you should seriously look into publishing these pieces," she told me after I let her read a few. To me, they were simply sketches of my jobs and the people involved, but the woman, who said her name was Sara (no H) and mentioned she worked at the English Department at the local university, thought otherwise. After discovering she was a professor, my gut dropped to my feet. I became intimidated and unsure of my writing, almost embarrassed that I had allowed a writing professor to read my scribblings.

"Look," she blew smoke from her small lips and held her red lipstick-stained cigarette between two thin fingers, "Just consider it. Don't sell your words short. Especially the hard words." She took her second shot of rye whiskey and left as I weighed her advice carefully, staring after her as her figure dissipated into the shadows of the parking lot. I thought about the douchebag author my dad took me to see years earlier and how I never wanted to be an author if it meant being like that man. But Sara gave me a gift of confidence that I didn't even know existed when it came to my writing. Would the world even want to read what I had to say? A tiny flicker of hope began to form, a small, tender flame that maybe the world of writing had room for someone like me too.

Dear Hillary,

Thank you for your submission. It takes a lot to have the courage to put words to paper, especially words that are so vulnerable. We appreciate your effort and thinking of us to send your work to. We gave the story careful consideration, and though we are not accepting it for publication, we hope you find a better fit elsewhere.

Thanks again for trusting us with your work.

Best,
Editors

Dream House

I found a safer job cleaning businesses, which allowed me to keep attending community college, where I met a woman in one of my classes who, in turn, introduced me to a man I would be married to for almost two years. It was a marriage constructed from immaturity as well as our codependency. A relationship hastily strung together, like a nautical knot loosely wrapped before an oncoming storm. I was twenty-one when I met Mike. It was a natural love, easy to fall in love in that high school kind of way. We had been together for almost a year and decided marriage was the next step because that's just what you do. You either break apart or commit. It never occurred to either of us we could be together, no next step. But at the time, there was no in-between.

We bought a house, another logical next step after finding a job at a local conference call company that paid a lot more than cleaning and offered health insurance. We began to settle into our new lives, our new roles. Looking back now, both of us had broken role models and no idea how to navigate a marriage or financial responsibility, especially at a young age. Both of our parents had been divorced for years, and our only examples of marriage involved confusion, fighting, and an eventual splitting apart.

The night Mike and I moved into our new house, the power went out for two days, and the septic tank exploded, flooding the basement in a slurry of feces and urine. It wasn't even our shit—it was the previous owner's shit—and we didn't know how to handle someone else's shit, let alone our own.

"Maybe we can cover up the sewer smell with pine tree air fresheners? Hang enough of them from the ceiling and walls?" he offered up sheepishly. We both stood on the basement steps, surrounded by stink and brown liquid, not looking at each other. I was waiting for my mom or dad, maybe even his mom or his stepdad, to show up and help us. No one came.

Being alone in the basement of our house reminded me of the time I had slept overnight with my Brownie troop in the local mall when I was eight. It was deserted, as if we weren't supposed to be there. The mall had shut down beforehand, but it felt like it had suddenly been abandoned during the end of the world. And had I blinked, I would have missed it, all while eating a pretzel from Wetzel Pretzel, distracted, tossing pennies in the water fountain outside of Claire's Boutique. I wanted my mother that night, not the Brownie Troop leaders, but I knew the other girls would tease me if I started crying. So, I held it in.

Upstairs, all our belongings crowded the rooms and hallways, clothing, books, and CDs, all packed in boxes, shifting from their weight. Inside my faded yellow 80's Barbie Dreamhouse, tucked in the corner of the bedroom, my long-lost relic of childhood, when I thought being married and owning a house was just part of being

a grown-up—snap your fingers, and you have a home! Snap your
fingers again, and furniture appears! I could see Barbie managed to
have all her furniture and clothes unpacked, so why couldn't I? I
thought about how Mattel set me up for failure by modeling Barbie
and her lifestyle as something to strive for, someone to *be*. Did I
really believe that anything was possible with the right outfit, a
perfect home, and a conforming partner?

We slept on the floor that night in sleeping bags, just like that
night in the mall when I was eight. The same need to have my
mother with me settled itself over me, heavy as spring snow. That
night, we both fell asleep without saying a word, and I learned to
curl inside of myself and far away from anyone or anything. I didn't
know how to make him happy, and he didn't know either. That
night I learned that even when you sleep next to someone, you can
still feel completely alone.

Rabbit Hole

After the imminent divorce from Mike, Steven and I started dating, and not long after, he moved in with me into the house Mike, and I had bought together. There's no romantic story involved in our meeting. We were friends first, then started spending more time together. I was interested in his mind and his music knowledge, the books he read, and his tattoos. His lifestyle. It was a smooth transition and bad timing, just coming off a divorce, but I didn't see this mistake at the time. We tried to pay the mortgage together by getting a roommate to live in the basement, a guy named Jared from where we worked together. The rent was always late, and his dog constantly shit on the carpet. After I found beer bottles in the shower, I was over it. I didn't want to be a landlord on top of everything else, so I put the house up for sale. There were too many memories, and it was time for a new start.

When Steven had first moved in, he insisted we cover almost every inch of the beige painted walls with posters of music artists and bands. Soon, the house looked like an angry teenage boy's room. I hated it, but I didn't say anything. I wanted your father to feel like it was his home, too, even if temporarily. He told me his idol was Ian Curtis from Joy Division, how he would have fainting spells for no reason and shake on stage as if having seizures. I found your father falling to the floor at random moments and lying still. The first time it happened, I was scared, worried that there was something wrong with him. But as I knelt next to him, I noticed his eyes darting under his eyelids, and he kept swallowing. I knew he wasn't passed out and began to understand that he was faking the spells to get my attention and sympathy. Each time he sat up after about 30 minutes, blinking, a confused look painted on his face.

"What happened?" he asked me. I would help him up to his feet every time, telling him, "You passed out again. Maybe you should see a doctor." But he never did.

"Doctors are bogus. Look at my dad. He's been dying from cancer for years. He should have been dead a long time ago."

The house eventually sold, and we moved into a one-bedroom apartment further into the heart of the city. We brought along my dog, Poo, who was still a puppy from my previous marriage, along with Swirly, who your father found as a kitten. Friends from work were supposed to help us move but wound up ditching us, so we took the entire day to move our belongings from the rental van onto the second floor of the apartment building. I hadn't told my parents about how I started seeing someone so soon after the divorce, let alone moved in with him. My idea of avoiding any issues was to keep everything a secret. Eventually, as the day dragged on and the sun continued to beat down on us as we moved each piece of furniture, one by one, I told Steven I was calling my dad to come to help us.

There was no way we could finish moving with just the two of us. Half an hour later, my dad showed up, confused as to what was going on, his lips a straight slash across his face.

"Dad, this is Steven. We're moving in together." We stood, surrounded by furniture and cardboard moving boxes as cars sped by on the busy road next to us.

"I can see that," my dad said, staring hard at Steven. He stuck his hand out, and they shook. "Nice to meet you, Steven. You guys need some help?"

He didn't ask any questions at the time, but I saw the look of concern on his face. There would be time for answers later, I knew. I felt myself hurtling down a rabbit hole I couldn't stop myself from falling into. I knew every choice I was making at the time was a bad one, yet I continued to find myself drawn to your father. He was every intriguing, bad boy in school I grew up with. Mohawk, leather jacket with band buttons, and he could sing like no one else I had ever heard. We spent our weekends at the local gay karaoke bar across from work where he would sing into the mic, everyone from the bar watching—the epitome of my teenage angst crush.

I was going to continue falling, not knowing if I would ever hit the bottom of the rabbit hole.

Sometimes They Can Be Terrifying

Security and financial security, I came to realize, were two entirely different things in the world of becoming an adult. After quitting the job where I met Steven for a position that promised me better money and the possibility of becoming a manager, the job quickly unveiled itself as a pyramid scheme. Out of desperation, I took a job working as a front desk administrative assistant for two career headhunters. I spent most days sending out fishing emails to prospective clients and greeting clients when they came in for their appointments, listening to The White Stripes, and poking around on the internet when the days were slow. Steven had also fallen for the pyramid scheme job but could not find work. We could barely live off my one income, which wasn't much more than minimum wage. My one boss, Dan, was older and wore a full suit and tie every day. He was balding with thick-framed glasses and reminded me of what someone who grew up in the conservative 50s would look like. My other boss, Sandra, a younger female in her late thirties, always wore skirts and blouses, never a full dress, and would sit on the edge of her desk smearing dark maroon lipstick on before a client was about to show up. I watched her carefully from my desk, noticing the way her high heels dangled off her feet, the way she flirted with her compact mirror as she smoothed the lipstick over her lips. I wanted to be like her: in charge, put together, sexual in a business-like sense. Months after starting the job, I was pulled into Dan's office, where Sandra was sitting in one of the chairs meant for clients, a look of pinched concern on her face. My stomach dropped. Dan shut the door and sat behind his glossy walnut desk with the octopus paperweight, something I always was tempted to steal but never did. Right then, I wanted to. They were going to fire me.

"Dan and I had a little talk, and we wanted to discuss with you our concerns about your attire," Sandra began, spreading her hands out on the chair arm between us as if proving to me she wasn't carrying any weapons. "We think that perhaps you could be dressing a little more professionally."

"Yes, more like Sandra, maybe?" Dan offered, struggling to find a way of not sounding sexist or condescending.

"Yes, just," Sandra was struggling to find a way of not sounding like a total bitch. I could see the fight on her face. "You know, more trousers—" Who the fuck called pants trousers? "and skirts. You know. Business casual." I looked down at what I was wearing, what I had consistently been wearing, which was always a combination of a sweater and the two pairs of dress pants I owned. Steven and I were not doing great financially, and I had no money to buy groceries, let alone new clothes for a job that didn't pay me enough money to survive. My parents were not a source of help either, both struggling with finances in their own lives. I had things under control, I figured. I didn't need anyone's help. I had this.

"I don't have any money to buy new clothes," I offered, staring at my boots that were already showing signs of falling apart.

"Oh!" Sandra started, her face lighting up as she took her hands back, this time to her chest. "The Goodwill! Or The Arc! There are so many wonderful thrift stores you can go to that have an amazing selection of work clothes. And thrift store shopping is so much fun!" I stared at her earnest face, then at Dan's face, which was trying to hold it together. It was clear he was uncomfortable with the conversation and didn't want to insult me. I appreciated him for that. Still, Sandra was completely unaware of the difference between thrifting for fun and thrifting to find clothes to keep a job that didn't pay shit. I no longer looked at her in the way I had before. I left the office with a promise to change my outfits by the next paycheck, but instead, I started using what I overheard them discussing with clients about resumes and interviews, cover letters, and job searches to land an interview with Ford Credit in the collections department. I knew the job could earn a lot of money, and I wouldn't be seeing clients. I would be on the phone in a call center, and what I wore or didn't wear wouldn't matter. I landed the job and told Dan one Friday before he was about to leave. He almost looked pleased, and I left without saying goodbye to Sandra.

Months went by, and my paychecks were enough, more than enough, to keep mine and Steven's heads above water. The work was horrible. I was being yelled at and insulted every day by customers, and I struggled. But the money kept me there, and I received a promotion from collections to the Skip Trace Team. It meant I would no longer be calling customers on an autodialer. It meant managing my own accounts. It meant not being screamed at every day.

☿

One Sunday morning, I was in the kitchen cooking bacon, a rare luxury food item. I placed the strips on paper towels and blotted them to get as much grease off. Swirly, our cat rubbed against my legs, trying to get my attention. I broke a piece off the tip of a bacon strip and gave it to her, which she quickly ate, licking herself after she had finished. I left the small galley kitchen to go to the bathroom, glancing at Steven, who was still sitting on the couch watching TV, before closing the bathroom door. As I flushed the toilet, I heard the sound of the water then, "Goddammit! Fucking cat!" followed by a small cry. I knew what was happening, and my heart felt as if it was being shoved into my stomach. I flung the bathroom door open and ran towards the kitchen. His back was to me, and I saw him holding Swirly in the air while he choked her, his hands enormous compared to her tiny neck as her eyes bulged, her small paws clawing the space between his face and hers slowly ceasing their movement. Her green eyes were glazed over. I knew that look. What it meant. There was a piece of bacon on the ground where she had jumped on the counter and grabbed one. His face was red, sweating, his eyes large and unblinking. Unforgiving. I was on personal terms with that look and aggression since we moved into the apartment.

I surprised myself at how fast I made it to the kitchen running from the bathroom, slamming into his back, slapping his shoulders, screaming to let her go. He dropped her like a hot potato, and she fell to the ground, heaving. I got down on my hands and knees and stroked her neck as she gasped and vomited bits of bacon.

"Ssshhh, it's okay, it's okay," I picked her up in my arms and ran past him, not meeting his eyes, not wanting to face what was inside him.

"Fucking cat. She's lucky I didn't kill her." He walked back to the living room as I shut the bedroom door to evaluate Swirly, who was trembling in my arms, claws digging in, refusing to let go of me. I should have left him right then, taken all the pets, and fled, but I had nowhere to go. I meticulously ran through every possibility in my head and knew I was stuck.

I didn't leave the bedroom for hours, contemplating my next move. I waited until Swirly's breathing had evened out, her eyes no longer dilated, and gave her some water from my nighttime water cup by the bed. She curled up on my pillow and settled into a deep slumber. I thought about taking her to the vet to be sure, but what could I have said? How could I have possibly explained what happened? I felt like an animal myself, trapped and scared, unsure where to go or what to do next. My mind was heavy, and I knew I had to leave him, not only to protect myself but to save my animals from what I knew he was capable of.

It all seemed so easy then, Son. It did. And beginnings, yes, they can be beautiful. But sometimes, they can be terrifying.

Suicide Cliché

I don't remember how many pills your father took, but it was everything that was inside the medicine cabinet. The night after he choked our cat, I told him that we should get our own places and spend some time apart. What I meant was I needed to get away from him. What I meant was he had already pinned me down, choked me, and kept me trapped inside of our apartment during arguments as I screamed for help, the neighbors completely ignoring me. What I meant was it was only a matter of time before he became bored with the animals and moved on to me.

He was lying on the floor, empty pill bottles surrounding him. If he were a painting, he would be called *Suicide Cliché*. I stood near the circle of pills, careful to not let my feet touch them, and told him I was moving out. He blinked up at me and said nothing, a blank look in his eyes, as he suddenly lifted himself off of the floor and ran, locking himself in the bathroom. I gave up even trying to discuss anything with him with an ounce of rationality and retreated into the bedroom, leaving the door cracked to listen for his footsteps. After a few minutes, he stumbled out of the bathroom like a broken mannequin and collapsed on the floor. Eyes closed, face puffy and pale. I was reminded of when we first moved in together when he would fake fainting spells for attention. Lie on the floor like a puddle of pay-attention-to-me until I gave in. But this time, I knew he wasn't pretending, understood immediately he had done something to himself. I called 911.

Steven was always good at control tactics. He often bragged about how he learned about these tactics from his father—a former green beret—the only time he ever talked with any kind of pride about him. My friends warned about his controlling behavior and offered to help me move out, but I didn't want to get any of them involved. It was embarrassing enough to know I had tangled myself into his snare. For years, many of the friends I had witnessed my quick divorce and move-in with Steven and had decided to throw down loyalties with my ex-husband. I knew Steven was trying to gain control over me to manipulate me, but at the time, I still saw him as a human being. I saw him as a life that needed to be saved. I saw him.

I should have let him die on the floor, Son. Choking and gasping, his face turning blue. His breaths shorter and shorter until nothing but beautiful silence. But you never would have been born.

The ambulance arrived, and I followed it to the hospital, only a short ride away.

They pumped charcoal into his guts, and soon he was sleeping, his dark hair pasted against his forehead, tattoos stark against his waxy skin. Someone from the billing department asked to speak with me, asked me his name, and if he had insurance, our relationship, where he worked. I told them his name was Derek Levi, and he's unemployed, and we were friends, that's all. I filled out the intake form with a false phone number and address. I told them my name was Anne. Because that's what you do when your boyfriend tries to kill himself. Cover for them. I might as well have been someone else, a different person altogether. I took him home early the following day, and he leaned on me as I got him into bed before I left for work.

"Thank you," he told me, eyes still watery, still blue—a sad ocean.

The room was a faded, ugly yellow. The sun had been in the process of rising as its beams slashed their way across the walls of the bedroom. Swirly meowed, and Poo whined. I would feed them before I left. Make sure they had what they needed. Walk the dog. I would feed Steven when I got home. Soup and crackers. Ginger Ale. Comfort foods, comfort blankets, comfort TV. I would take care of him. I would take care of everyone. How could I have left when everyone needed me? That would have made me a monster.

Approximately one-third of female homicides in the United States are accompanied by domestic violence, and that number is increasing. Another—less well-known—issue pertains to suicide risk and suicidal behavior related to abuse between intimate partners.

Intimate partner violence may constitute physical, sexual, or psychological harm upon a current or former partner or spouse. In these situations, offenders try to control their victims through fear, intimidation, threats, or force. Perpetrators may humiliate their targets, control what they do, withhold information, isolate them from friends and family, and deny access to money or other basic resources[vi].

[vi] *Intimate Partner Violence: A Pathway to Suicide*
https://leb.fbi.gov/articles/featured-articles/intimate-partner-violence-a-pathway-to-suicide

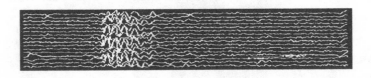

White Knight Syndrome is defined as "people who enter into romantic relationships with damaged and vulnerable partners, hoping that love will transform their partner's behavior or life."

I can save you, Son. I can take you away from him. I am The Knight[vii].

[vii] If the Knight of Swords is on your side, you basically have nothing to fear for there is no mightier opponent than him. He will literally fight to the death for you and no one stands a chance against him.

The Knight of Swords is all about actions and the intellect. He does not care nor leave any room for feelings and emotions.

https://www.tarotparlor.com/blog/knights-of-tarot-meaning-messages

Dear Hillary,

Thank you for sending us your work. We appreciate the chance to read it because we believe that making art is such a daring, wonderful act.

It's difficult for us because, despite the number of great pieces we receive, many of them don't quite fit into our editorial needs. We're glad you thought of us, though, and hope that you'll submit to us again in the near future. We truly enjoyed reading your work. We receive too many submissions to make individual comments possible, but we do wish you luck in placing this with another magazine.

Thanks again. Best of luck with this.

Sincerely,
The Editors

au·ra

(in spiritualism and some forms of alternative medicine) a supposed emanation surrounding the body of a living creature and regarded as an essential part of the individual.

The Empress

Only a few days after I started my new job position, I found out I was pregnant with you. I thought of you as "baby," and I didn't want to know your gender. It didn't matter to me, I loved you immediately, and I didn't even know you. I drew seahorses in my notebook during work. Felt you curl and uncurl your tail inside of me.

I didn't say anything to anyone at work about being pregnant for a month. I was worried about losing my job or being demoted to collections because of my pregnancy. I was still in disbelief. Steven and I lived in a one-bedroom apartment on the north end of town, close to Chapel Hills Mall and work. He was unemployed, hadn't worked in months, sitting at home watching TV with our pets.

I grabbed my Tarot deck and pulled The Empress card. She was beautiful, stoic; calm energy surrounded her. She was everything I was not. The clock on the wall ticked, counting down. The two parallel lines on the pregnancy test indicated a positive, not negative. I took the dog for a walk. Smoked a cigarette.

Am I strong enough to raise you on my own? What kind of man will you be if I do?

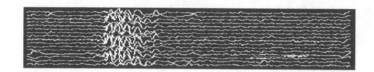

I thought about raising you with a monster you would soon call
daddy. I hoped a son would make him happy. Christmas Eve, he
would hang our stockings over the fireplace, *Daddy Baby Mommy.*
He would do this so I would know he was the man and you were his
and I was his too.

Steven was in the dining room, categorizing his CD collection.
There are stacks of CDs scattered across the apartment. He told
me it's best to arrange them in autobiographical order instead of
alphabetical order, like John Cusack's character in the movie *High
Fidelity.* I hesitated, knowing I could wait to tell him. I thought about
Seattle, how I was so close to moving there. How close I would be
to the ocean if I had gone. How cold and crisp the air and the water
would feel surrounding me. But this was before, and now there was
no going back. I placed my hand over my lower stomach, hoping to
feel the red glowing heartbeat.

I know how cold the green sea feels. It's so cold it burns when you touch it.

 **A Spell to Protect Pregnancy**

Write a magic square on brown paper:

S A T O R
A R E P O
T E N E T
O P E R A
R O T A S

Place inside your bra, your purse, your wallet. Any place you can carry this spell with you always.

Remember this is a vulnerable time. Remember a child's soul is still cradled within your own. Has not yet placed feet on this earth.
Devils aren't the only evil waiting for us.
Sometimes they are the people we trust the most.

Tony, the Kids Are Here

Steven told me about his parents, how they lived in a trailer park east of town, how it was a nice trailer park. He said "nice" like he was describing a vacation home. *Nice.* He never wanted me to meet his parents before, until just then.

One Sunday, before you were born, we drove to the trailer park before I knew I would be leaving him. It was nice. The homes all had small lawns, some with gardens. Tiny white dogs jumped from behind miniature white picket fences, pricier cars parked out front. We pulled up to a home with a black 4Runner parked out front, and before I could get out of the car, a woman was running from inside the trailer, hands splayed out in the air, eyes wide. Her hair was jet black and cropped short in a pixie cut, big dark eyes, olive skin.

"We finally get to meet!" Her nails are long and manicured, painted a rusted pink. She had a heavy Long Island accent.

"Nice to meet you," I told her, and she pulled me to her, squishing me against her large breasts, which were covered by a black leather jacket.

"Leave her alone, Mom," Steven said, slamming the car door shut. She waved a hand at him, "Oh, stop." Turned to me, "Come on in!"

The three of us stepped in succession inside the house, which was dimly lit, save for a giant television screen emitting light onto a man sitting on a couch in the living room. He was holding a Coors Light and watching a football game on TV. "Damn!" He slammed his beer down. "Damn! Offsides my ass!"

"Tony, the kids are here."

I stood awkwardly in the living room, waiting for an introduction. Tony didn't stand up, though I could tell he was taller than Steven by the way his legs stretched out in front of him. He let out a huge burp, pounding his chest with his fist.

"Carmela, get me some chips." He said, staring at me, then at Steven, eyes resting back on the TV screen. She moved to the kitchen and grabbed a bag of Lay's potato chips, pouring them into a red plastic bowl.

"You kids want anything to drink?" Carmela asked as she ushered us into the kitchen, past Tony, who had already dismissed us.

"Now I remember why I didn't want to come here," Steven said, grabbing a soda from the fridge.

"Get her one, hon," Carmela called out, already opening the door to the fridge again and pulling out a Coke. "Here, hon," she handed me a can of soda, and we made our way into the living room, finding a seat on the leather couch next to Tony, who continued to ignore us as he watched his game on TV.

"Carmela! Get me another beer!" Tony lifted up his empty beer can and shook it, eyes never leaving the TV. Steven once told me his dad had been dying from cancer for years. The man I saw sitting on the couch didn't look like he was dying. Then again, death comes with many different faces. He had a full head of dark brown hair, plump cheeks, light blue eyes just like Steven's. Tall and slightly overweight, just enough to see a beer gut forming. He had a particularly feminine look to his face that was hard to dismiss. Once, Steven and I discussed our childhoods during one of those intimate moment conversations.

"My dad was a Green Beret living in Germany with my mom. One night, he got so angry at her he started beating her. He beat her so badly the MPs came and busted the door to their house down and had to pull my dad off my mom. She was in the hospital for a week after that. Three broken ribs, a collapsed lung, two black eyes. The works. He really did a number on her, and it wasn't the first time. My childhood, growing up, typical. He doesn't even need alcohol as an excuse to beat her up. It's just him. He's evil. He has no excuse for his hatred. That's just who he is."

There was a movement from my left as Carmela continued to fire a series of rapid questions at me, ignoring his demand, wanting to know where I'm from, where I work, where my family was. Tony had bolted up from the couch, a move I didn't think he was capable of at the time, and stood over Carmela. She stopped talking, right in the middle of "Where did you go to–" and lowered her head immediately, eyes to the floor.

"I. Said. Get. Me. Another. Beer. Bitch." Spit formed on his lips. Her eyes remained locked to the floor. "NOW, Carmela. Move your fat ass!"

I glanced at Steven, who said nothing, a smirk on his face. Carmela moved past him like she was avoiding open flames from a fire and ran into the kitchen, pulling a beer from the fridge and handing it to him with a shaking hand as he regained his seat on the couch, lowering himself slowly. He popped the can open, taking a loud slurp, then burped. "Penalty," he said, gesturing towards the screen with the can. Carmela ran into the bedroom and shut the door slowly to emphasize she wasn't, in fact, slamming it. Steven finally looked at me, the smirk even bigger, and said:

"I told you. Now you know. My parents are monsters."

Monsters are real, Son. Sometimes we don't have to reach too far out to touch them. Sometimes they're right in front of us.

Real

On April 20th, 1999, five years before you were born, I was training for a job with Deluxe Checks, a local check and paper printing company in Colorado Springs. A large TV hung on the wall, flashing the local news across the screen. I watched as a rabbit hopped on the lawn outside the window, noticing how far back the lawn stretched to the parking lot all the way back to the warehouse building. The rabbit was tan and white with a small tail and legs bigger than its torso. It reminded me of *The Velveteen Rabbit*, a story I loved as a child. After enduring a short life of pain and heartbreak, the rabbit becomes real at the end. The lesson is: if you suffer long enough, you become real. My thoughts were interrupted as another employee in the class lifted her hand and pointed her finger at the TV screen.

The other employees in the room gasped and cried out. My eyes followed the fingers to the TV screen, and I watched as Columbine High School, just forty-five minutes north, was swarmed by police. A news helicopter flew over, and its camera swept down at the school. The body of a boy appeared on the sidewalk leading up to the front door, face down, arms at his sides, as if he'd become exhausted and stopped to lie down—a crown of blood formed on the concrete around his head. The camera panned toward the police as chaos broke out in the parking lot. The audio of a viewer calling the news station. A worried mother, asking if they know if her son is alright. Did they have any information about the children who managed to escape? A list of names? Who's alive?

The following day, I drove to Columbine and parked my car on the side street. A large group had already gathered at the school, and memorials had been erected. I walked to the empty parking lot, where a single vehicle was left sitting in a spot. It belonged to one of the students killed. Inside, on the passenger seat, was a hair tie and an unopened can of Coke. Her odometer read only 4,998 miles. Sometime during the night, the mourners placed 15 wooden crosses alongside the grass in front of the school with each name, including the two teenage shooters. Later, this would become a point of contention, and two of the crosses were quickly removed. It never became apparent if the two crosses were placed alongside the others in the confusion of the body count, or if, even for a moment, someone felt that the two boys responsible for the massacre, along with their terrible decision, also needed to be mourned.

The burning candles and the pictures of the dead, the piles of bouquets and stuffed animals, formed a world of its own amongst the wooden crosses. The odor of decaying flowers hung in the air, the sick, sweet smell of memory. Grief is capable of hanging in spaces between death and life. The sound of wailing cut through the air like a tornado warning, quiet at first, then gained ground as the small group of mourners turned into a crowd, continuing to swell as the sun gathered itself in the sky. A picture of a student pinned to a cross, a smiling face now still and at rest, another body in the morgue. I wondered about the boy I saw on TV, how I watched as his figure lay motionless as the choreographed chaos of the police and news crews moved around him.

Earlier, when I turned my head away from watching the rabbit, I saw the boy on TV and willed him to get up. If he stood, it would all be okay. This wouldn't be real. But he remained motionless. He was in the morgue too, and I knew his name. I knew all of their names, including the two teenagers responsible. When I focused my eyes back on the lawn, at some point between the massacres unfolding on the screen and when I initially glanced away, I saw that a car had smashed the rabbit on the black asphalt of the parking lot. A crown of blood surrounded its head, eyes open, and stared in my direction.

If you suffer long enough, you become real. I know that now.

Lifesaver

The old wives' tales are true, the women in my office insisted. They cackled and suspended a pendant over my stomach. If it swings in a circle, you are a girl. If it swings back and forth, you are a boy. They tell me that the chain should hang with the expectant mother's wedding ring. I gave them a cherry Lifesaver.

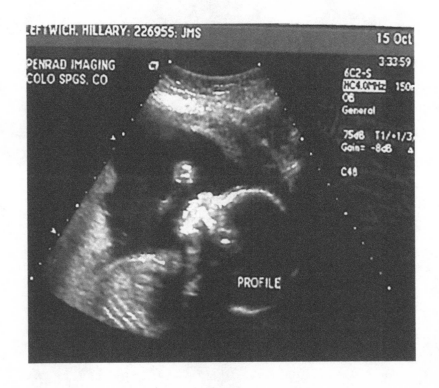

Whatchamacallit

Your father and I are in the car while I drive us to Walgreens after watching a movie. We had started a slow process of ghosting our friends that almost went unnoticed during this time. At first, it began with him talking shit on my friends, little things that planted a seed and made me question my friendships.

"Anna loves to talk down to you. Did you notice that the last time she came over?"

He was spending more time working as a manager at a local music and apparel shop in the mall across from where we lived. He had plenty of social interaction, but I did not. I mainly spent time with my mom—who was not a fan of Steven. Being a woman automatically made her an expert in men's bad behavior, and she wasn't about to let her guard down with him. All the close friends I had before I got together with Steven had all but deserted me after my divorce. Complex loyalties are hard to predict when it comes to shared friendships. I knew I was becoming isolated and lonely, but I also had our animals to keep me company, and you were going to be a physical presence in my life soon, and I planned on focusing all of my time and energy on you[viii].

We walked inside the Walgreens, talking about The Cure and their albums and what years they came out when what started as a fun conversation turned into an argument. A switch that only took a second to occur. It always only took a second.

These switches began happening more and more as my pregnancy turned from weeks into months. It was late evening, and there were only a few people inside, but your father continued to angry-whisper at me, the tone he used to scold me when we were in public. Loud enough for me to hear him, but no one else. I walked up and down the aisles, forgetting why we even stopped, pretending to look for something I couldn't find. My fingers were tentative as they tapped the different colored boxes of candy I loved as a kid: Whatchamacallit, Dots, Likamaid, Nerds. I picked up a Whatchamacallit and headed towards the cashier.

"*Pornography* was released in 1980, then *Seventeen Seconds*[ix]," he told me, blocking my way down the aisle with his body. I nodded, not meeting his eyes, knowing it was useless to disagree. He was making the angry-nervous gesture he always did when he would get ready to explode, a combination of biting his nails then curling his hands into fists.

I managed to slide past him and walked to the next aisle, looking around to see if I could get myself close to another person before

---

[viii] Social isolation is systematically controlling who you see and/or who you talk to and/or who you receive phone calls, messages or email from. Controlling where you go so that you become socially or geographically isolated from other people.
  dvconnect.org.

[ix] *Pornography*, the fourth studio album by The Cure, was released on May 4th, 1982 by Fiction Records

he escalated. He was behind me, following at my back, his mouth against my right ear.

"You stupid cunt, don't walk away from me. You know I'm right. Why do you even bother arguing with me? If you make a scene, I swear to Christ I'll fucking stab you in your pregnant stomach right here like a slab of meat. You hear me? You listening?"

I walked to the photo counter, my face numb, heart slamming inside my chest. A young guy behind the counter with long, dark hair tied back in a ponytail. My heart dropped. I was hoping for a female employee who might have understood my silent fear and called someone to help. I approached him anyway, my eyes locking on his. I was fully prepared to have the police come and take him away, fuck the consequences.

"Can I help you?" he asked in a half-bored, half-forced tone.

Help me, I mouthed before placing the Whatchamacallit on the counter between us. I noticed the name tag on his shirt said, *Joey.*

"What?" Joey asked, leaning forward. It was too late. He was behind me, hands on my back. "Hey, there you are! Let's go, babe. It's getting late. You done here?" I handed Joey a dollar and change, the quarters shaking in my hand, wondering how could he not see what was happening? Did he know and just didn't care? All I could do was nod while he stared at me like he missed something, but he couldn't figure out what. I didn't break my gaze with him until your father's hand grabbed my candy bar and pushed me towards the doors.

"Have a good night!" Joey called out after us, waving a stiff, bored hand in the air.

Womb

When I am alone with you, I spend hours thinking about all of the things we'll do together, what I can teach you, my escape plan, just in case things don't work out the way I am hoping they will with your father. You adjust and readjust your body inside of me, turning, fluttering. I knew we would have a special bond. I could already feel a connection with you that mothers have felt since the beginning of time—an ancestral womb.

I stretch myself out on the couch and put the headphones on either side of my stomach. I play Nina Simone, Lauryn Hill, and Otis Redding. My favorite song to play for you is "Sitting on the Dock of the Bay." The sound of the waves as he sings about leaving his home in Georgia for San Francisco reminds me of my failed secret escape. I read the song was released only after Otis's death, which makes me love it even more. A secret song, all his own, recorded somewhere in a dark studio made of rich wood and gold fabric. His voice rolling off rounded walls as he sings of the sea and a loneliness that won't leave him alone. But he has his chair and a dock to sit on, and I have you. I have you, and I have Fight growing along with you inside me.

You are my chair.

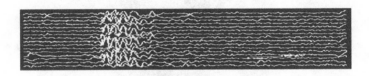

Wandering womb was the belief that the uterus could move freely about the body and was the cause of hysteria in women in ancient Greece. An "animal within an animal" was the culprit for a wandering womb, which is also cited as the source of witchcraft in trials.

Am I an animal within an animal? What then, Son?

How Close the Lightning Is

You were two days late, and I was ready for you to come out. Two months prior, my skin began to show the scars of stretching my skin to accommodate your body in mine. How does it feel to have another human inside of you, some of you might ask. It's a detached feeling, almost as if you are a balloon and a string is pulling your head into the sky. You watch as the clouds smear by you in beautiful puffs, knowing that floating this way will eventually end when your body reaches the earth's atmosphere and the sun burns you up until there's nothing left. In other words, I was terrified of the pain of giving birth.

My stomach was becoming a bloated extension of my body, a watermelon-sized growth on my mid section I had to constantly haul around. I was unable to tie my shoes, get up from a seated position, had to push my seat back in my car to accommodate the growth, and I was ready to burst. My supervisor at the time, a late twenties-early thirties woman with an athletic build, often stared at me with frightened eyes.

"Do you have a lot of stretch marks? I can't stand the thought of my skin being ruined by stretch marks." I blinked at her in disbelief. This woman—a veteran of the army, a marathon runner, someone who appears to have such strength—detested stretch marks, a right of passage, a badge of courage that marks us as women coming into our womanhood during puberty, during pregnancy. I couldn't believe it. It was the first time anyone made me aware of the attitudes and pressures of our society when it comes to women's bodies during pregnancy. I recall my mom's own stretch marks. How I always traced them as a girl with my fingertips, marveling in their silver sheen. I didn't answer her. I couldn't. My stretch marks on my lower abdomen were mine and mine alone to marvel at, which I often did—tracing the lines with my index finger like brushing paint on a canvas. To me, they were beautiful, a marking of courage and an ancestral line of womanhood. I could never look at anyone's stretch marks and find them ugly or frightening.

I searched articles online about women who go way beyond their expected due dates and what happens to them. My friends told me to relax and let nature take its course, but I was becoming anxious.

I booked an appointment at an acupuncture clinic after reading online that labor can be induced this way. The night before, I tapped on the pressure point on my ankle, another way to start labor. I sat in the lukewarm water, my belly a slick, glorious balloon blocking the view of my feet as I tapped at the spot the article said would work. I expected that night to start feeling what I imagined were the shooting pains of beginning labor, but nothing happened.

The next morning, I sat in a treatment room with a petite Asian woman who smiled down at my belly, pointed at my shoes, told me to take them off, and said she would be right back. She closed the door behind her, leaving me to contemplate the large table covered in blankets in front of me where needles would soon be poking into my body. I was bending down to untie my shoes, struggling to find a way to reach past the circumference of my protruding belly, laughing again at my inability to do even the simplest of tasks, when I felt something wet between my legs. For a moment, the thought of your body pressing against my bladder and causing me to piss myself crossed my mind. But no, that couldn't be it. I stood up slowly and opened the door, peeking out to a full waiting room. I waddled-ran my way past the other patients who sat in chairs while flipping through magazines and into the women's restroom, slamming the stall door behind me. I tugged down my maternity jeans and panties and sat on the toilet, waiting for something to happen. I didn't have to pee. I knew my water had broke.

Pulling up my panties and jeans, I walked quickly out of the bathroom and approached the front counter. The same woman at the front desk who checked me in glanced up at me, a look of concern crossing her face.

"I'm in labor," I told her, "And I need to leave my appointment."

Her mouth formed the perfect O, and she covered it with her index and middle finger as if to stop it. "We need to call an ambulance!" She spoke low, which I am grateful for. I didn't want the entire waiting room to know what was happening.

"I'm okay," I assured her, patting both sides of my shoulders as if she needed physical proof of me standing in front of her for it to be true. "I'm going to drive myself to the hospital."

This time her mouth opened, and she gasped, "No, no! I need to take you then!"

I was already spinning in my head what needed to be done when I turned away from the counter, hoping she would let me leave without pushing help on me. "Then let me follow you in my car at least, so I know you get to the hospital safely." She was already grabbing her purse and whispering to her coworker, who eyed me up and down as if deciding on how pregnant I could possibly be. She nodded, and the receptionist grabbed my hand as we walked out the door to the parking lot.

I called your father at work and told him I was in labor and going to the hospital. I started the Jeep, buckling myself in, and noticed more and more water was leaking from me. The car seat was soaked. There was no odor, but from what I read and heard about in the birthing class at the hospital, there would be eventually. Steven told me he was on his way and hung up, not bothering to ask how I was getting to the hospital or if I would be driving myself.

It was late morning, and traffic wasn't heavy. The receptionist followed behind me like a spy trailing another spy who's out to destroy the world. I was the other spy. When we pulled up to the emergency room doors, I shut my engine off, and she was already opening my door and offering her hand to me. My hands shook. I hadn't had time to process what was happening, just that my entire crotch and legs were wet, and I was alone with a woman I didn't know who was kinder than any stranger I had ever encountered. She led me inside to the check-in desk and waited as I told them my water broke, and I was pretty sure I must be in labor. The nurse at the front desk sat me in a wheelchair, and we both looked at the woman from the acupuncture office.

"Is she with you?" The nurse asked, nodding towards the woman standing in front of us.

"No," she said, "I was just making sure she got to the hospital safely. I will go now."

I grabbed her hands and squeezed them in mine. "Thank you," I told her, forcing what I knew was fear in my eyes to leave for a moment as I reassured this woman that I was going to be alright. She squeezed back, then broke away, walking out the door. The last I saw of her was a dark swoosh of her braid and her two red Nikes as she left the hospital. As I was wheeled into the back, a part of me longed for her presence, knowing what was waiting for me in the following hours.

There are three stages of labor: early, active, and transition. I was only dilated three centimeters when Steven appeared in my hospital room. My parents and stepparents hadn't arrived yet, and his parents weren't there either. It was still early in the game, the nurse kept informing me as she took my blood pressure and temperature. She was an older woman with a gray-streaked bun and cat eye glasses. I was in the "Early Labor Phase," which lasted until a dilation of three centimeters, but since my water already broke, this put me somewhere between early and active labor. I was terrified of labor pains, which had already begun, a dull ache combined with sharp shooting pains in my abdomen and lower back.

Steven had my hand in his while the nurse ran through the information on what was happening to me with him and what stage of labor I was in. He nodded his head as a look of concern or frustration altered his face. He squeezed my hand as he asked all the right questions. Satisfied, he thanked the nurse, who smiled quickly at us before leaving the room, telling me she would be back to collect a urine sample from me in an hour. The door clicked shut, and Steven pinched my hand until I cried out. I waited for him to say something as he began pacing the space in front of my bed.

"What the fuck were you thinking?" He whispered, face purple-red. "Driving yourself to the hospital after your water broke? Are you fucking stupid? Are you insane? You could have killed our son before he's even born!"

The cramps in my pelvic area were becoming stronger. I turned my head to the machine next to me, measuring and recording my contractions; the frequency and intensity looked like spikes and soft, rolling green waves on the chart. I was reminded by the nurse to count from the beginning of the contraction until it ended and to keep track of how long each one lasted.

Count the number of seconds after the lightning flashes and stop when you hear the thunder's rumble. Divide this number by five. This is how close the lightning is to reaching you. Listen, it's coming.

☿

I was stuck in a hospital bed in labor with a man who would be screaming at me if not for the nurse's station down the hall, leaning over me, face swollen with hatred, fists clenched, and I was terrified. There was no one to help me. I kept seeing the woman from the acupuncture office, her dark braid swaying against her small back as she walked out the automatic doors of the emergency room. I wanted to be with her, her hand clasped in mine, walking out the doors together. Somewhere, there was an alternative version of me living a life without fear. I get coffee with friends and gossip. I go to school and graduate. I get a job doing something I love. Somewhere, I am living a good life with my soon-to-be son, and we are happy and safe. I wanted the woman I was supposed to be back. I wanted to be that woman I was supposed to be.

"I'm getting something to drink from the vending machine," Steven told me, pushing himself away with his hands from my bed and clicking the door shut loudly behind him. I had five minutes to myself, tops, and with the way my labor pains were being timed, another ten minutes before the next one hit. I needed to use the bathroom and couldn't wait any longer. Pulling the wires off attached to me, just as the nurse showed me to do earlier in case I needed to get up, I unhooked the IV bag to take with me as I walked into the bathroom. I sat down on the toilet and peed for what seemed like forever, taking deep breaths, forcing myself to stand up again when I finished. I looked at myself in the mirror and saw a face I didn't recognize. *Is this me? Really?* I was pale, eyes bloodshot, lips thinned out, and everything else was bloated. Less than a year ago, I was almost in Seattle. Almost to the cold, green sea my dreams were saturated with. I chose to stay and raise a baby with a man who was terrible to me. I made a mistake. But I knew it wasn't too late. I knew I still had hope, and I could somehow fix all of the wrongs I had done to myself. I had to.

I heard the door open and shut, "The fuck?" and I opened the bathroom door. My hand gripped the IV stand as I stepped out.

"You're supposed to give the nurse a urine sample, remember?" His face was in front of my face, and I could count the number of tiny black dots lining the iris of each blue eye. I heard a woman down the hall screaming, and a man shouted, *CAN SOMEONE HELP HER? SHE'S IN LABOR!* I heard a woman in another room laugh and say, "Anyone need anything from the cafeteria? I hear they're serving tacos."

It was rush hour on North Academy Boulevard, which ran parallel to my hospital room. The cars were driving by and stopping at the stoplight, speeding up, slowing down, speeding up, slowing down. The pain in my abdomen, pelvis, and back intensified, and I doubled over in pain, my eyes focused on his black and white Converse All-Stars with the black laces he bought, saying white laces get dirty, and he didn't like his shoes looking like they were dirty. It took him an entire hour to lace his shoes precisely the way he wanted them. *Just right,* he said, patting the laces.

I needed to count to keep my focus on anything but him, and the only thing stopping him from hitting me was the fact that we were in a hospital together. I remembered my breathing exercises from our parenting class at the hospital, pulling all the air in the room into my lungs, then pushing it out again.

Onetwothreefourfivesixseveneightnineteneleventwelvethirteenfour-teenfifteensixteenseventeeneighteennineteentwenty

The next contraction hit me hard, and I doubled over, but Steven was still standing, loudly whispering or quietly yelling, and all of the words fell to the floor in separate pieces like a puzzle torn apart:

Bitch

   Never listen   *kill our kid*

  Tests to be done   *stupid*

    Selfish cunt *Not about you today*

 weak bitch *Die* *Can't you hold it?* *I swear I'll*

There was a buzzing in my ears. I watched his shoes to see if they moved towards me, reminding me of the hallway in junior high at CSC, of Paul standing over me, offering me his slick, warm hand, of my complete surrender and obedience to him, not just to Jesus. I wanted to be surrounded by women, a circle of womanhood holding me up, feeling their hands on me as each contraction hit, knowing they know what I know—a universal connection passed down through generations—a never-ending circle. I wanted my *sisterhood*. But I had none.

The door to my hospital room opened, and the nurse with the gray-streaked bun stepped inside. Steven reached down to help me up, the same copy of "Worried Face" he forced on his face earlier reappeared.

"Oh, boy, what happened? Did she fall? Is she okay?" The nurse rushed over as they both assisted me back to my bed.

"I'm okay, I promise," I told her, feeling both ashamed and embarrassed over the attention.

"She was on her way back from the bathroom after I stepped out for a minute, Nurse. I know she was supposed to give you a urine sample, but she had to go. I'm sorry if she messed up any tests you needed to run. I guess she just wasn't using her brain." He rolled his eyes.

The sheets on my bed were incredibly white against my skin. I smoothed them out over my legs, thinking of buttercream frosting on a wedding cake. I would never share a wedding cake with this man.

"Oh, that's okay. We can get a sample later. It isn't a huge concern." The nurse patted my hand as she attached the wires monitoring my contractions. "How is your pain level, sweetie?

Okay?" I nodded. "And what are we at now? Are you keeping count?" I nodded again.

"Ten minutes," I told her.

"That's good. A lot can happen in ten minutes. They should start to go down from there. Just remember to keep counting and breathe. Use your breathing exercises together. Make sure you help her, okay, Dad?" She shut the door behind her, and we were alone together again.

"Breathe on your own, bitch," he told me, settling himself on the small chair next to the bed as he pulled his phone out. "And don't fuck it up, think you can handle that?"

The silence between us was a wolf pacing the floor, waiting. The sound of the heart rate monitor beeped fast, the pulse of a rabbit's heart as it runs in terror from its predator. Even faster, if you can believe it.

What to Expect When You Don't Know What to Expect

You were born during the early morning hours on a cold February day by an emergency cesarean.

You were supposed to weigh seven pounds but surprised everyone by weighing in at 9 lbs. 1 oz. When they brought you to me on the operation table, naked and screaming, you looked at me, and I looked at you, and the world froze. My beautiful Pisces child. I was now responsible for another human being and well-being. The thought never crossed my mind (at the time) that your life would be in danger. It was a moment for connection—the ancient, enduring bond between a mother and their child—a bond that can never be broken. Even in death. In a cold hospital surgery room on that February day, you became my savior, and I yours. I knew I would give anything it took, including my own life, to protect you.

Steven stomped inside of my hospital room. "Damn dog won't take a shit," he shouted.

The words bounced off the walls. It was spring and twenty degrees outside. I was stuck at the hospital for at least another two days, and I couldn't save my dog from this man. Less than a year later, I would give my dog away to provide him with a better chance at survival than he had with me. There were many deaths I experienced while being with Steven. Watching him abuse my animals, animals I had before I met him, felt like he was killing me along with them.

The nurses had all been fighting over who got to hold you. They nicknamed you "Peanut." They were touching you more than I was able to, and I was jealous they were able to hold you more than I was. They told me there would be time to bond at home.

Steven didn't stay at the hospital long. He was working at the mall and was always on call. I worried about the animals and how they would take to you. They were alone in the cramped apartment. The pregnancy book I was reading, *What to Expect When You Don't Know What to Expect*, told me to bring home a blanket with your scent and allow the animals to become used to your smell. I had already unraveled the knit blanket my boss's wife had made, unable to eat or focus. I wondered when they would discharge us. In the hospital, we were protected.

The nurse brought you in so I could breastfeed. You were wrapped tightly in a blanket, and I could only see your face peeking out. I tried to nurse you, but it hurt.

"It will take a few days to get used to it," she reassured me. Steven sat in the chair across from my bed, whispering to someone on the phone. It was probably another woman, but I no longer cared. I had you. A scent cloud of baby powder and cotton surrounded you. Every time you yawned, a soft squeak followed. Even at two days old, I could tell you would look exactly like him. I wondered how I could love you so much when you looked like someone I was terrified of.

I heard him talking. A dog was barking itself hoarse. The nurses walked by in the hallway and giggled; their voices drowned out by the sound of a gurney being wheeled outside of my room. The sound of metal rolling against tile reminded me of cold ocean waves.

I'M A BOY

BABY Leftwich   RM# 18

MOTHER Hillary

DATE OF BIRTH 2-20-04   TIME 0033

WEIGHT 9 lbs 1 oz

LENGTH 20 inches

HEAD 14 inches

BABY'S DOCTOR Sliger

MOTHER'S DOCTOR Letch

The Birth Center

3205 N ACADEMY BLVD., COLORADO SPRINGS, COLORADO 80917 (719) 776-3486

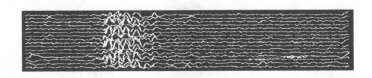

When the plans had been made and the airplane ticket bought. When Seattle becomes a word evoked by a higher power. When the images of a cold ocean and damp sea moss can be spun into a blanket of comfort and hope. When unknowingly becoming pregnant throws a choice in your face you are forced to reckon. When you say goodbye to possible oceans and remember how cruel mountains can be.

While looking down at the two parallel lines in a small window of a pregnancy stick and seeing an ocean within the blue. To consider an unborn child into a child born. To decide between freedom and life.

The Pacific Ocean's tides impact Earth by shaping it slightly, a few inches. The rise and descent of a mother's labor impacts the dilation of her cervix leading into childbirth. Each peak and collapse of my contractions remind me of the ocean I likely will never see. An ocean ruled by ancient gods—not goddesses. But to me, each rolling wave speaks of womanhood, of motherhood. Giving of everything we have within us as the tides push. Pulling back our gifts as if to say, *don't give someone all of you when they take everything from you.*

They say babies can instinctively slow their heart rate and breathe underwater in what's called *bradycardic response.* Most babies know to hold their breath in water as if the connection between the amniotic fluid has yet to be forgotten. As if we could, if we wanted, return to our wombs and forget the world that will kill us.

In Colorado, there are no oceans, no bodies of water, or damp driftwood crisscrossing rocky beaches. Here, I am all mountains and dryness. Scorching summer sun and sharp pine needles. The smell of wildfires, burning aspens, and the sounds of animals dying. We are miles above sea level with acrid skies and no rain. No tides or salt or seaweed. But we are made of water. Perhaps one day, I will return.

Mother- *The Latin root matr: mother, ancestress.* A woman from whom a person is descended. To give up her own life, to give life, to give of life. To surrender to tides as they push and pull, give and take. I dream of oceans the color of seabeds and mermaid tails. The lull of the waves rocking me like secret lullabies. I dream of an ocean that is too distant and too cold to touch. Of goddesses ruling the waters and repossessing their tides, leaving behind nothing but broken shells and heavy stones no one will ever be able to carry. To hear their voices, still within the broken waters, as if to say, *slow your heart, hold your breath, and one day, you will return to me.*

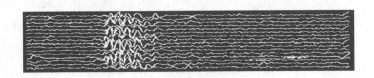

In ancient Babylon, lullabies were used as magical charms, meant to protect sleeping babies. But darkness pervaded across cultures and centuries, with lullabies expressing fears directly or metaphorically about absent fathers, injured, sick or lost children, domestic abuse, and unhappy lives.

I sing to you the lullabies that babies have heard for centuries. But without sadness or fear. There have to be moments, Son, and memories made where we are happy. When it's just you and me. I sing:

You are my sunshine, my only sunshine
You make me happy when skies are gray
You'll never know dear how much I love you
Please don't take my sunshine away

The other night dear, as I lay sleeping

I dreamed I held you in my arms
But when I awoke, dear, I was mistaken
So I hung my head and I cried.

Happy Family

Somewhere, although I don't remember where now, there is a portrait of us taken at Sears or one of those department stores located in a mall now abandoned. I went to Kohl's and spent money we didn't have on a nice dress for me, a tiny suit for you, and a dress shirt for him. The photographer's assistant posed us as *Happy Family:* Father, mother, child. Our hands braided together while I held you in my lap. The Nuclear Family as the mushroom cloud began its bloom behind us. We are smiling the smiles of the fated—his hand on mine, the same hand he used to threaten me. My hands cradling you. The same hands that protected you from him.

What does it mean when we talk about a mother's love? To have the heart of another growing inside of you, the body of another feeding off you. To protect this life above anything else. Maybe a mother's love is the final act before the world collapses—the one pure existence left in a world full of devastation.

The photographer said, "Say cheese."

What I wanted was a photograph to transform us into a family. The root for family comes from *famulus,* "servant." To be a family is to be a servant to him, both mother—protector—and a lightning rod for his wrath, a distraction from you, absorbing his hatred and anger. I read the statistics on domestic violence and death and how more than forty percent of all homicides of women involve their spouse or partner.

Maybe that is the role of women. To be the lightning rod for men. To connect the umbilical cord once more. Our bodies act as ghost ships, empty vessels to carry the hearts of the men we will serve or protect. Never both.

The photographer said, "Say cheese, one more time."

Flash.

A Fucking Women's Shelter Cliché

My mom told me not to tell anyone I was pregnant until I was at least four months along. She said I was still within a time period where I could miscarry, so best not to say anything, not just yet. But I knew you weren't going anywhere. When I pissed on the end of the pregnancy test stick, missing some because I was so nervous, I sat with my bare ass still hovering above the toilet, watching the clear window of the test stick like my dad would watch the football game on TV. When the second line appeared, I knew it would be just me and you, those two lines like two trees standing parallel together, our roots feeding off one another for stability.

I chose to tell Steven the news, and he seemed happy. He said that this was the kind of new start we needed to get our shit together, then went right back to sorting out his CDs as if I had just told him that I was going to the mall to run an errand. So, I did. I left and bought a light blue baby blanket with a teddy bear on it, trying to imagine the baby that would soon be wrapped inside of it.

"Fuck if you didn't go and fuck up your plan to move to Seattle," my work friend, Carla, told me over the phone. "So, how did this happen?" I had my bags packed and a ticket to Seattle before knowing I was pregnant. In between the flashes of his perfectly even teeth and fists like cartoon anvils, there was the ghost of Seattle haunting me with comforting smells of earth and moss from the green surrounding a waterfront city.

"Carla, I don't know." I gripped my cell phone and bit my lower lip. "It's a surprise for sure, but I have to try to make it work." Carla made a noise like she was getting ready to throw up. "You sound like a fucking Women's Shelter Cliché."

He came into my hospital room the day you were born, his face all red and lit up like a red-hot tamale, and told me the dog was going nuts and pissing all over the carpet, and he couldn't get it to go outside. I had problems of my own, like trying to get you latched on to my nipple—either nipple—didn't matter. Every time I tried and failed, a new nurse was replacing the other nurse (they all looked the same: short dark hair, big bosoms, baby blue hospital scrubs) as they leaned over to tell me to keep trying because it was *the best thing for the baby*. But when the room was silent and dark, and everyone had left after bringing their flowers and stuffed animals, I held you and stared at you for hours, soaking you in. Your nose was shaped like a tiny pear placed perfectly on your face, and your lips had the same Cupid's bow as mine. New babies have a smell of milk and baby powder hovering around them like a tiny cloud, a perfect scent. All I could think at the time was, *this is the boy who will finally save me.*

Steven showed me your room on my first day back from the hospital. We had just moved into the new townhouse months earlier in preparation, a townhouse I bought under my name only to ensure no financial ties with him. When I had left three days before my acupuncture appointment, the crib was set up with butter cream-colored sheets and an animal mobile dangling over it, the elephants and lions looking anxious to do their spinning duty. But as I stood there and looked around, I noticed the room's previously bare walls were covered in black plastic-framed posters of different bands. It looked like a teenager had moved out the night before, and a crib was shoved in the room as an afterthought.

I said nothing when he asked me what I thought of the decorations and placed you into your crib. I had become used to saying nothing. The Silent Woman. You looked up at me and belted out an angry scream. He sighed and told me, "There's no way in hell that baby is crying like that all night. I have band practice and work in the morning," he sighed loudly, pointing at me with his index finger. All I heard was him telling me I could either figure out how to get you to shut the hell up, or I would be sleeping in the crib with you. That night, I rocked you in the rocking chair in the corner of your room, your head nestled perfectly under my chin, making tiny noises and barely moving like you were still inside of me. I stared at the mobile hanging above your crib, thinking about all the other babies in the world right now that were staring up at the same animals dancing above them as they slept, and wiped away the tears spilling down my cheeks only after they started wetting the top of your head.

No one had told me at the hospital, or maybe they had, (they give you so much information when you've only had two hours of on and off sleep that it's impossible to retain anything), after giving birth and a prescription of heavy pain pills it was likely constipation would happen. I bundled you up and strapped you in the car seat, driving the six blocks to Walgreens. I carried you while still strapped in your baby seat and hooked on my right arm, my purse, and my baby bag on the other arm until I found the laxatives. I had never taken a laxative in my life and had no idea what to buy. I read the different boxes and settled on one that would act the fastest, then threw in some maxi pads (I was bleeding as if my entire cervix had erupted from the inside) and paid. That night, relief finally came. But then, you started having diarrhea, something I hadn't been told was normal for a newborn. I read the laxative box and froze. I was breastfeeding. Anything that went through me went through you. He came home just then, dropping his guitar case and noticing the look on my face and the box in my hands.

"The fuck is that?" He yanked it out of my hands, staring down at it, laughing. "You backed up there, babe?" He threw the box on the coffee table and coughed into his hands. "Smells like shit. When was the last time you changed his diaper?" I knew better than to say anything back, so I took you into your room and changed you for the second time in thirty minutes. I started to panic. The laxatives were still in my system, so I couldn't breastfeed you. He came into your room as I was still changing you, the box in his hands. "You aren't supposed to take this shit when your breastfeeding, you stupid bitch." He threw the box at me, hitting me on my nose. "That's why he's shitting so bad. He's only been alive for five days, and you're already killing him!"

You were still laying on the changing table, pumping your legs like you were riding an invisible bike, trying to escape. I didn't blame you. The first push landed me against the wall, and my head whipped around, so I was staring right at a poster of Iggy Pop's wrinkled face. My stitches from the C section burned, and I grimaced, covering my head with my arms, my hands gesturing towards the changing table. I told him, "Watch the baby." to make sure you didn't fall off the changing table. He laughed, and there was a thud. It was hard to judge the weight of the noise, and I was in a position where I could still move my chin up so my eyes could see past my arm, but I felt sick, and I didn't want to look.

"Call the doctor, you stupid bitch, and find out what you need to do." I heard his feet padding across the carpet and out the door into the bedroom, where the door clicked closed. I jerked my head up and unraveled my arms and saw you were still laying on the changing table, still riding your imaginary bike, and looked down and saw a huge box of diapers that he had pushed to the floor.

"You can feed him. Just don't take any more laxatives." The doctor sounded annoyed on the phone. I had called the hospital and had him paged, and now he was probably pissed off that he had to take a phone call during his dinner. Maybe his wife decided to make his favorite dish, and he was just sitting down when his pager went off. "Fuck if it isn't another frantic, paranoid new mom again," I imagined him telling his wife, her breasts, not engorged with milk, appearing perky in her new Gap sweater. I imagined that all doctor's wives wore Gap sweaters and spent hours sipping coffee at Starbucks and discussing which recipes in *Food and Wine* were best paired with which wines, going home to husbands, and having the best sex ever, followed by hours of cuddling and tenderness. "You didn't take enough to affect his system, and he needs the nourishment," he continued. "If he still is having bowel movements every thirty minutes through tomorrow morning, call my office and bring him in first thing." I thanked him and hung up the phone, staring at you while you practiced opening and closing your fists, making popping sounds with your lips. Later that morning, the shit-a-thon stopped, and you were still the happy baby I brought home from the hospital. I felt like a deflated balloon, wondering how many other mistakes I would make. Did other mothers fuck up as bad as I had? Why weren't more women talking about it, if so? I grabbed your two chunky legs and helped you bike pedal as I sang an Elton John song to you, "Rocket Man," and how we would fly away into space together and never look back.

Bastard Child

A week after you were born, your father took you to the mall. It was a Friday night, and a cold front had just moved in. I tried to tell him not to take you—you were still a newborn and susceptible to germs and being hurt—but he wouldn't listen.

"My coworkers want to meet him," he said, wrapping you in a blanket and slipping a hat over your head. I knew it wasn't enough layers.

"Well, what if I stopped by with him tomorrow? I can buy you lunch even," I slipped on a pair of extra thick booties on your feet, purposely distracting him, knowing I wasn't going to win this battle.

"From the pizza joint?"

"Yes, whatever you want." I placed you inside another extra warm blanket and wrapped it around you—cocooned in insulating fabric and fluff.

"I'll take him tonight, and you can stop by tomorrow so everyone can see him. Not everyone is on the schedule tonight," he picked you up, his keys dangling from his pocket, slamming the door behind him in a puff of cold spring air.

It wasn't the first time in the past week he'd taken you from me. After we left the hospital, he dropped me off at our place and brought you to see his mother and father without me, claiming I needed more rest. He took you from me to Walgreens to get more diapers rather than leaving you at home with me. He made it seem like he was helping me by giving me time alone, but it was intentional. He did it to hurt me. To isolate me from you.

During this time I began to experience feelings of severe depression and irrational thoughts. Thoughts that you didn't need me, you were better off without me. This was fueled by my suspicion that your father was cheating on me with a coworker in combination with him taking you from me, leaving me alone with my thoughts and swollen breasts, staples from a C section, and burning pain from where I had been cut into.

I wanted to kill myself and didn't know who to talk to about my feelings. Your father had managed to isolate me from my friends, and I didn't want to burden my family with my emotional upheavals. I already knew I had made a mistake by staying with him because I had become pregnant. That a child never is a resolution for any relationship troubles, especially the violence I had experienced at the hands of your father. I didn't realize I was experiencing Postpartum Depression[x] and I needed help. But I couldn't help myself. I didn't know how. I was overwhelmed with a constant fear he would take you away from me. I lived in a constant state of paranoia and depression, swinging back and forth like a janky pendulum, never

[x] Postpartum depression occurs in 10-15 percent of women in the six months following childbirth, with risk factors often mirroring those typically found with major depression.
  https://www.henryford.com/blog/2019/06/baby-blues-vs-postpartum-depression

deciding which direction to go. I was fucked up. A useless, saggy-stomach milk-breasted woman.

At the mall, I sat on a bench outside the store where your father worked, a blanket spread over us as I nursed you. The bathroom was too far away, and I was tired, and you were hungry and needed to be fed. An older woman walked by and stopped in front of me. Her giant gold cross dangled between us as she pointed her finger in my face.

"Sinner!" she hissed.

"What?" I asked her, pulling you closer to my body.

"Exposing your breasts in public! Whore!"

"I'm not exposing my breasts; they're covered by a blanket, and I'm trying to feed my baby. That's what breasts are for."

"You're going to go to hell, you know that, right? And your baby won't have a mother. Your baby will be a bastard child."

I'd had enough. With little sleep, depression, wondering when or if I'd be able to find a safe daycare to watch you when I had to return to work in two months, protecting you from your father who was behaving recklessly towards you by carrying you around and showing you off to friends and coworkers like you were one of his collectibles with no regard to your safety. Now this woman, in this Christian town, with all of the boldness and self-righteousness in the world, pointing her finger at me and calling me a whore was too much for me to handle. I stood up, my mouth a snarl, a mama bear ready to kill[xi].

"Get the fuck out of my face! All I'm doing is feeding my baby and minding my own business! Get the fuck away from me!"

[xi] Some of the symptoms of baby blues are irritability, fatigue, and sadness. PPD symptoms are often more severe and include aggression, extreme stress, and potentially feelings of detachment from the baby.
https://www.henryford.com/blog/2019/06/baby-blues-vs-postpartum-depression

People raced towards us as the woman cried out with all of the might of The Lord himself within her, and your father was suddenly there, having seen the commotion from inside the store, and started pushing me away towards the exit doors. It was cold and snowing outside, and I expected him to give us a ride home after closing the shop. He nudged me out into the early evening air, pacing back and forth as he often did before deciding what punishment he was going to lay down, then stopped in front of me as I continued to hold you close to my own body. You were still suckling as if nothing was happening.

"You stupid bitch! Are you trying to get me fired? Why didn't you go to the bathroom like all of the other millions of mothers out there who breastfeed? You can't breastfeed in public! Are you trying to cause a scene? What were you thinking? Walk the fuck home, walk home! Give me my son. Give him to me now." Red hot anger pulsed through me like a volcanic heartbeat. As if I would hand *my child, my baby,* over to this man.

"He's with me, he's staying with me, you have to work." he cracked his knuckles and began pulling you away from me.

"I'll finish watching him while Leah closes. You fucked up. You better hope that lady doesn't file a complaint against you."

Then you were gone with him, vanishing behind glass doors and fluorescent lights, and I knew there was nothing I could do. If I went back inside, he would sabotage me. Want to destroy a mother in a matter of seconds? Take their child from them. I turned around and started walking to the bus stop, the sting of angry tears freezing against my face. I couldn't keep up the charade of Mother and Partner. I knew I couldn't. Something was going to give, and either way, you were going to be hurt in the long run, no matter what the outcome.

au·ra

An event that can manifest as music, swirling colors, a memory, a sense of impending doom, a smell or taste, a rising nausea, or an intense sensation of déjà vu. A warning.

A Spell to Drive Out the Epilepsy Demon

"a mouse and a shoot of a thornbush' on the patient's door; an exorcist dressed in a red garment and cloak; a raven, and a falcon."

A spirit who makes him unable to speak

Moonstruck

Lunatic

Possessed

Mommy Mannequin

Your first word was *Da-da,* followed by *Mama.* In several books on parenting, I read that these are usually the first words spoken by babies because it's easier to say the "D" sound than the "M" sound. Still, I was disappointed. One day, I pretended to be the tickle monster with you—a game I invented when you played inside your bassinet. I pretended my hand was a monster, hiding and tickling you, which drove you into fits of adorably cute giggles, your face lighting up. My entire world was filled with you and sunshine and pure happiness. You opened your mouth, and I thought, *this is it, he's going to say his first word!* and I was already mouthing "Mama" when the word came falling out of your mouth, a clear, undeniable *Da-da.* I sat in a moment of hurt but seeing your silly face and the grin you were showing me, as if to say, I'm talking! and the hurt passed. It didn't matter what your first word was. You were talking, and that was to be celebrated.

There were moments when your face would twitch, and your eyes would roll back into your head. I became worried and took you to your pediatrician immediately, who assured me if they were seizures, it wasn't anything to be concerned about just yet.

"Any history of seizures in the family? Maternal or paternal?" he asked.

"Paternal, his father's mother had seizures growing up, but she grew out of them. Nothing serious."

"Ah, yes, sometimes stress can cause seizures, but if it's a childhood-onset, he may well only have one or two and never again. Or he could just grow out of them. Keep a close eye on him and bring him back if you see him having any more incidents."

There were no more face twitches, and after six months, I knew it was time to start crib training you. You were getting bigger, and you needed your own space. I read about crib training from several books published by various pediatricians. The method I decided to try involved slowly stepping away from the crib one foot per night until you made it to the door, at which point you were to leave. The pediatrician who recommended this technique advised it would be a difficult journey. I figured it would take me about a week to train you to sleep in your room on your own.

The first night was terrible. Worse than terrible. When people talk about new parents not getting any sleep, they aren't joking. I remember my grandfather talking about sleep deprivation POWs were subjected to and wondered if it was anything close to what I was feeling at the time. After feeding, I placed you in your crib, which you viewed as more curiosity than an actual bed. Your mobile dangling over you with shapes of crescent moons and stars, animals and clouds, with sprigs of lavender and angelica for protection spinning sweetly as a slow lullaby softly tinkled in the room. I covered you with your favorite blanket and handed you the stuffed elephant you loved. Everything was set. I knew I would have to stand at your crib, smiling down at you but not picking you up. The next night, I would step one foot away from the crib, still not picking you up, even if you were screaming. The next night, this would continue until I made it to the door, at which point I would leave the room. The goal was to have you sleeping in your crib, knowing you were safe in your room, and I was there with you as you closed your eyes.

But things didn't go as I planned. As I stood at your crib, a look of confusion crossed your face when I didn't pick you up. Your crib was fascinating at first, sure, but after five minutes, you wanted nothing to do with it. You held your arms in the air, waiting for me to pick you up.

"Mama! Mama!"

You started to cry when I didn't pick you up from your crib. I stood stoic, still smiling a forced smile, hands at my sides. A perfect mommy mannequin. After thirty minutes of crying, your face red and covered in tears, "Mama!" I relented and picked you up. Exhausted, you fell against my chest and began hiccupping. One minute later, you were out.

This continued until after three weeks, I managed to make it to the door of your room.

When you closed your eyes that final night, a feeling of pure accomplishment flooded over me. I had done it. Not only did I know I was doing what was best for you, but it was a parenting goal achieved as well, one that many parents on the online forums complained about not being able to achieve. As I stood at the door, still smiling, still feeling the joy spread through my body, the doorknob turned, and your father was in the room before I could stop him.

"What the fuck? Are you going to let him cry all night? Not my son! I take care of my son!"

Before I could stop him, he pushed me out of the way and headed over to your crib, startling you from your sleep and cradling you in his arms as if shielding you from some invisible monster.

"No son of mine is sleeping alone in his room when he's still so young. My mom tried to pull that shit with me as a baby, and my dad wouldn't have it either."

I watched, too stunned to move, as he took you out of your room and into our bedroom. I felt all the hope I had of living with your father as long as I could begin to leave my body. He set you down and turned, running towards me. Before I could think, he shoved into me, and I fell to the floor. He stood over me, yelling, the words not even discernable. I got up and scrambled like an animal into the bathroom and slammed the door behind me, locking myself in. Shaking violently, I felt for the cell phone I knew I had pushed into my back pocket earlier that night. I felt the hard feel of plastic and let out a shaky moan as I dialed my mom's number. My stepdad, Jeremy, answered the phone, and I told him I was locked inside my bathroom, and he needed to come over right away. I knew I had no control, not even over you, and there was nothing I could do to protect you other than to leave. I heard you crying and started to open the door, then a pound.

"Get the fuck out of the bathroom now! Get the fuck out now!"

"Don't you hurt my son! Don't you dare fucking hurt my son!" POUND. My heart. The door? POUND.

After what felt like years, my stepdad showed up, using his spare key for emergencies to let himself in. I heard him talking calmly to your father through the door, the same calm tone I remembered him using on my older brother when he was acting up when we were teenagers. I heard footsteps, then the front door opened and slammed shut. I waited; my breath held in until I thought I was going to explode.

"It's okay to come out now," My stepdad said, and I rushed to open the door. He stood in the hallway holding you in his arms, and when you saw me, you reached out your hands, face squished as you started to cry. He handed you over to me, and I hugged you as you snuggled against my face, all the strength left inside me dissolved.

"You're not his son," I told you, my breath catching in my throat. "You're *my* son."

Remnants

Babies are exposed to several toxins, such as life-threatening poisons like lead or other heavy metals, both in utero and after being born. By the time they are breastfeeding, the toxicity level in their bloodstream has already caused enough damage to produce permanent effects.

Environmental factors that aren't included in studies include fear and the threat of danger, which causes adrenaline to flood the body's system, forcing it into a fight or flight reaction. Fight or flight reaction leads to panic attacks and the possibility of anxiety disorders, including PTSD.

There are no studies on the impact of adrenaline on a fetus while in utero or present in breastmilk while a baby is nursing[xii].

Do you have remnants of my fear inside you, Son? Your seizures acting as a transference of terror. Could I have done this to you?

[xii] "Toxic Chemicals in Breastmilk" *Business Insider*, 2019

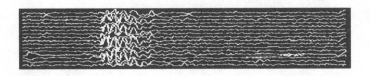

Christmas Eve, he hung our stockings over the fireplace.

Daddy

Baby

Mommy

The stockings didn't hang straight. He had a hammer to fix the crooked nails. He had a hammer to fix me too. I ran out of the house to the parking lot with you cocooned in my arms. There were cracks in the walls of the house we left along with him. Cracks replaced the broken picture frames that fell to the floor. Cracks he put there with his fist, with his hammer, with my head. I locked us both safe in the car. He followed, mouth a snarl, finger pointed like a Doberman's snout. He shouted that I was kidnapping you. The neighbors crowded around my old Jeep Cherokee, slamming their palms against the windows. Somewhere down the block, the ice cream truck played a happy jingle, and I laughed at the timing of it. Someone called the police. I unlocked the car doors when the cop beckoned me to come out. They handcuffed your father, shoved him in a police car. "Twenty-four hours in a holding cell," the cop told me.

Twenty-four hours to disappear.

Dorothy

She spills her guts: glitter and stale water, all over my hardwood floor. I clean up every piece of her, shards of glass, a half-cracked figurine of Dorothy. Her lips are red. A color my ex would call *Whore Red*. There is a look of anxiousness painted on her face. I pick her up delicately—because she is broken—and hold her between my thumb and forefinger. She is staring off into the abyss of my living room. A living room filled with moving boxes. I recognize the look, a look of waiting for the storm, the smell of incoming rain. She is facing the single event in her life that will change her path forever. An evil old woman is pumping her legs on a bike, a tornado scraping itself together, heading right for her. There were never Styrofoam flakes masquerading as snow in this fragmented globe, just glitter and plastic. Without snow, what do I call her?

When I stood in line at the women's shelter, my face painted on with the same look, a baby in my arms, and my lips smeared with my Whore Red, no one knew what to call me, either.

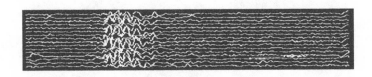

I saw myself in the hallways of the shelter. A different version of myself, a put-together, happier version, with shiny hair and fresh face, and you in her arms, happy and content. They were both alternate versions of us—a Should-Be Mother and Should-Be Son. Ghosts refusing to leave, a reminder of all of my failures and bad decisions. Still, despite the jealousy of the figure of me in the hallways, she haunted me, mocked me. Once, a purple lollipop in her lipsticked mouth as she made a gun out of her hands and pointed it at me, mouthing *POW!* Should-Be Mother was a sadistic bitch. She rubbed in how bad I was and how I alone got myself into the mess we were in. I failed on every level that society defined as a "good mother." By definition, by repeated mistakes, by the records shown, I was Bad Mother.

A fight or flight reaction takes about an hour for the adrenaline to wear down. When prey is in the act of escaping a predator, the adrenal glands become stimulated, causing increased heart rate, rapid breathing, and higher blood pressure. Our body's way of giving us everything it has in the moment of possible death. A final attempt at saving itself. A Hail Mary[xiii].

[xiii] Hail, Mary, full of grace,

the Lord is with thee.

Blessed art thou amongst women

and blessed is the fruit of thy womb, Jesus.

Holy Mary, Mother of God,

pray for us sinners,

now and at the hour of our death.

Amen.

A Spell to Bind Someone Upon Escaping

To place a freeze on someone, write the person's name on a brown piece of paper (a torn-off section of a lunch sack works perfectly). Fold it three times away from you. Place inside a plastic sandwich bag. Fill halfway with water. Repeat three times:

I bind you from harming me and harming my son.
I bind you from harming me and harming my son.
I bind you from harming me and harming my son.

If we had to leave again, I would take the bag with me, keep it frozen forever. I would not allow the water inside the bag to melt. I would not allow his name to float to the top like some kind of curse. How a name can evoke a fear that becomes a living thing—sent to destroy.
I would not allow him this freedom.
I drown his name along with my fear.
I drown him.

Another Man

Disrupt: interrupt (an event, activity, or process) by causing a disturbance or problem. I was all about tiptoeing my way around people and situations. I never wanted to cause any disruptions in other people's lives because of my poor choices. It isn't always easy to live within the space of your decisions, hoping that one day, you can move into another space, a much bigger area, occupy that area, and not feel timid about taking up space that you earned after feeling small for so long. These desires to live fear-free, stretch your body out further and further into more space, are terrifying, can you understand? Maybe, these desires will kill you. One taste of an orange-colored sun in an empty house, void of the monsters who have been chasing you for so long, is worth it. How many times do we have to die before we decide death, in the end, is worth the risk?

After staying in the women's shelter and constant calls from your father, I dropped the restraining order and moved back in with him. He still had keys to the townhouse and had been staying there, despite the order, because I wasn't there. Abuse is circular, in that sometimes it's a cycle that never ends, even if that circle becomes broken. I have no excuses for returning to him or the violence he created. It was easier to give up than get family or friends involved and possibly hurt. All I knew was it was harder to find help and a safe place than to just give in and return. Sometimes a safe house is no safer. Sometimes a restraining order makes it worse. Stokes the flames. I was in more danger, I felt at the time, running from him than I was staying put.

There is no justification for returning, Son. I didn't know. There's so much I didn't know.

Right around the time you started to walk, I had to give our dog Poo away. Your father threw him by his collar down the stairs several times, claiming he was biting him and going for you too. But my dog wouldn't have gone near you, and he might have bitten your father, but only to protect you. I knew if I kept Poo in the house any longer, something terrible would happen to him.

I found a family on Craigslist looking specifically for a Beagle and met them at a park nearby with Poo in tow. I watched them play and interact with him, and after an hour, I said goodbye to the dog I raised as a puppy, one last remnant of my previous marriage. There are no words to describe the pain of letting something you love go to save it. It's the highest form of love you can feel, and I mourn all my animals to this day. I try not to regret my decisions, but I find myself going back to blame and loss and grief all over again. I miss my animals terribly. Even now, the pain I feel is a knife twisting in my gut, ripping my insides out. No therapist has ever been able to help me heal the wounds from the animal abuse and loss I experienced. Even today, I can't watch a show or see a commercial with animals being harmed. I have become hypersensitive to the cruelty humans inflict on animals. It's a wound that will never heal, and any image or sound that reminds me of what I witnessed, what I couldn't stop, is a reminder of a life that put its trust in me to protect it, and I failed. I failed miserably, and I can never sew this seeping wound shut. It's the punishment I have assigned to myself. The only way to move forward is to spoil the hell out of the animals I have now with all the power of every crazed animal lover you see in the PetSmart shopping aisles.

By the time your father met Heather at his new job at a local printing company, I knew it was only a matter of time before he would leave me. I couldn't have been happier. Steven loved to have everything lined up, even his personal items so that nothing was out of line. Everything had to be arranged just so. His shampoo and conditioner bottles, shaving items, and toothbrush had to face a certain way. Even the kitchen storage containers, salt and pepper shakers, items in drawers, and especially all of the pictures on the walls had to be straight, even. But nothing had to be clean or even washed or wiped down, just *neat*. Tidy. Perfect. The bathroom sink could be covered in toothpaste bombs and hair, and it didn't matter, as long as the toothpaste tube and toothbrushes were lined up side by side with the same amount of space in between. I can't count how many hours I spent checking all of the spaces between our items to make sure they were perfect, or I wouldn't hear the end of it. Even his partners had to be aligned, including Heather. Having found out about his past affair at his job at the mall along with a sexual harassment charge, he had to quit or be fired. I wasn't surprised about either accusation. I had my suspicions all along. When he found his new job and started talking about Heather nonstop, I encouraged him to attend the employee parties and get-togethers. We had been sleeping on separate sides of the bed for the past year, and most nights, he fell asleep on the couch downstairs, not even bothering to make an appearance. When Christmas rolled around, he was barely home, and I had all the time in the world to share precious time with you.

We played on the greenbelt behind the townhouse, or I wheeled you down the sidewalks in your red wagon, filled with your favorite stuffed animals as you chatted away about what you saw around you. Since you first said "Da-da," none of your words had anything to do with your father.

When he finally told me that he was having a relationship with Heather at work, I feigned hurt and told him he needed to get the fuck out. His passion for me, for us, and his fire to control us had been simmering since we moved back in together. I refused sex, refused touch, and kept you close to me at all times. I was slowly saving money from my job at Ford Credit and planning something. I didn't know exactly, but I wasn't planning on staying in Colorado Springs much longer if I could help it. I knew we needed to get out and get far away.

"With what money, and where do I go?" He asked after I told him to leave. I knew he wanted to be with his new girlfriend, but he needed me to help him. If it meant getting him out of my life, he could have whatever he wanted.

The first thing I did was push everything off of the counters and shelves, desktops, and tables. I needed the perfection destroyed. We were not perfect, I was not perfect, and now we were finally breaking apart from each other. I stood, a satisfied grin on my face, as I surveyed my landscape of destruction. I felt vindicated for a small moment. Fuck him and his control overkill. But I knew to get him out for good, I had to ensure he didn't have any excuses to keep coming back. So, I gave him everything I owned. He took the TV, the computer, and most of the furniture. By the time he moved into his one-bedroom basement apartment with Heather, my townhouse was an empty skeleton. But these were just things that could be replaced, and the terror he had inflicted on us was at an end. Or so I thought.

☿

I met Alex on Facebook while he was attending CU Boulder for his BA in English. A tall, dark, tattooed poet from New Jersey with an accent and street hustler attitude that seemed charming and magnetic at the time. I fell hard and fast for Alex in a way I hadn't experienced since junior high. I was in love with him the minute I met him, though I could never admit it to myself. I hadn't felt lust or anything remotely close to it for years. Being with Steven had numbed me in ways I could never rationalize, even to myself. The post-baby body and losing the weight was harder than I thought it would be. My breasts were not my own for a year while breastfeeding. The thought of entering the dating world again was depressing and daunting. But Alex was not a petty man and didn't hold back when it came to commitment or our passion for each other. It had been years since I had felt myself even wanting to be intimate with anyone. I was so consumed by fear and exhaustion. Our first night together was a blur but ultimately sealed our commitment to each other. I was reminded of my own salacious desires that had long been forgotten, remembering when those feelings were once regarded as a sin and how hard I fought to keep my own inhibitions alive.

All witchcraft comes from carnal lust, which in women is insatiable. There are three things that are never satisfied, yea, a fourth thing which says not, It is enough; that is, the mouth of the womb. Wherefore for the sake of fulfilling their lusts they consort even with devils. More such reasons could be brought forward, but to the understanding it is sufficiently clear that it is no matter for wonder that there are more women than men

found infected with the heresy of witchcraft. And in consequence of this,
it is better called the heresy of witches than of wizards, since the name is
taken from the more powerful party. And blessed be the Highest Who has
so far preserved the male sex from so great a crime[xiv].

Throughout my five-year relationship with Alex, we became engaged a total of two times, both times at my insistence. Maybe I loved the idea of us as a family more than anything. Despite it not working out between us because of my demand for a commitment from him he wasn't ready for, he encouraged me to go to college and get my BA, something I wanted to do but thought I wasn't cut out for. He encouraged me to keep writing, to not listen to the people who assumed I wasn't a "real writer" and couldn't possibly ever become a writer as a single mom and with no education. Years later, Alex would share his writing assignments with me from his MFA classes at Rutgers after starting his first residency, showing me examples of writing from authors I had never heard of. I practiced, feeling unskilled and stupid, but he kept challenging me. Alex was not a typical student, moving from Newark to Boulder to get his BA and forming alliances with several writers. It was his dream to become a published author and teach. Whether he fulfilled his dreams or not, his support for writing knew no bounds. Because of him, I found my voice in a world where no one could possibly recognize me as a writer.

Sometimes good things come out of something that failed you, Son. It's
important to find moments of goodness, even if you feel like everything
is falling apart.

[xiv] *https://www.debunking-christianity.com/2013/12/i-have-never-read-more-anti-woman-text.html*

Alex had almost no reservations about me being a newly labeled single mom, and five months later, I had made plans to sell the townhouse and move in with him. It couldn't come fast enough. Leaving Colorado Springs behind was something I didn't want to wait for. The home I had tried to build for you was a failure, I was a failure, and I wanted to leave behind the ghosts of my childhood and your father and move on to better things, to give you a better life. To prove to you, I could be a better mother. I wasn't just a fuck up, I was a fuck up improving upon my fuck ups. Adaptable. Adept. My only mistake once thinking it had to be through another man to do so. Years later, I would kick myself, and kick myself again. Do we ever get past kicking ourselves because of our past mistakes?

A verbal agreement was made to bring you down to Colorado Springs every other weekend to stay with your father. With his newfound interest in Heather, I knew that having a child around wasn't in his best interest. He had no issues with me having you almost full time, paying for your medical insurance, food, clothing, and making things as easy as possible for him. Swirly was adopted by my mom. I wasn't happy about leaving her behind, but the apartment I had found with Alex didn't allow pets, and there was no way I could leave her with a stranger. Alex and I settled into a life together, and he took to you as easy as anyone can in a new relationship with a single mother. Still, I felt a foreshadowing of something to come, something restless about Alex that couldn't be defined just yet. It never felt completely permanent being with him.

atch me grow

My firsts

I slept through the night

__Four months old__

My first smile __Two months old__

I laughed out loud __Three months old__

I rolled all the way over __Four months old__

I could sit supported __Six months old__

Watch out! I began crawling __Five months old__

I spoke my first word __Da-Da__ It was __8 months__

I first clapped my hands __Six months old__

I took my first steps __Easter Day 2005__

I first learned to dance __1 year old__

I was able to sing along __1 year old__

My first favorite tune was __"Clean up Song"__

Traffic Was Terrible

Your father was late. He dropped you off every other Sunday after spending the weekend with you, and he was late. My thoughts flew to the worst-case scenario: kidnapping, murder, or he was in jail again. Alex tried to calm me down, telling me I was overreacting. I watched outside the window, unmoving, standing still as a mannequin as each car drove by. The sun was setting, and he was an hour late with no texts or phone calls. My body was full of live wires, and I shook, thoughts of him hurting you—my world destroyed and devastated—of having nothing left without you, my hatred growing stronger and stronger. I was filled with a fire that was unstoppable. Alex stayed away, feeling my burn.

I was readying to call the police when your father pulled up and parked on the street in front of our apartment. My body froze and then drooped as I felt my weight pulling me to the floor. All of the air and the life inside of me had escaped through the bottoms of my feet, and the room around me spun like a drunken spinning toy top. I wanted to throw up. Alex headed downstairs to get you, seeing me, seeing my collapse, knowing I would not be able to handle confronting your father. I heard him say from the street below,

"Traffic was terrible," then Alex mumbled something in reply. When he handed you to me a few minutes later, a look of concern on his face as I crumpled you against me, I shook my head at him, my silent words screamed, *do not tell me I don't have any ground in jumping to assumptions with this man. Do not tell me I have no right to think he would hurt my son. I love you, but do not tell me I am being paranoid. I am filled with a fear and a rage you will never understand.*

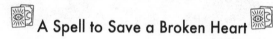 A Spell to Save a Broken Heart

Take a whole lemon and cut it in half. Scrub yourself down with the lemon while speaking your intentions of removal and protection.

Back of neck.

Shoulders.

Heart center.

Solar plexus.

Palms of hands.

Soles of feet.

Forehead.

Scrub in a clockwise motion.

While you scrub, remember all of the times they hurt you. How your heart became a bruised thing–swollen and tender–how it can survive outside of its body, still beating, even when the body has died. The Tin Man was gifted a new heart. Remember you are still here despite this death. Your body stands cold and rigid. No matter.

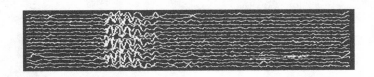

You stood in the hallway at a quarter til midnight, your hands two balled fists at your sides, the stuffed Dalmatian, "Doggy," on the floor at your feet, as your eyes rolled into the back of your head. You seemed to see me, even without your eyes, because you turned your head towards me:

Mommy, I'm going to die.

Some ancient sources interpret the sense of déjà vu experienced by those with temporal lobe epilepsy positively as a kind of prescience or precognitive ability that allowed people with the "falling sickness" to predict the future.[xv]

[xv] *https://www.thedailybeast.com/the-mysterious-case-of-the-demon-epilepsy-tablet*

Warning

I can't say this will be an easy letter, but I feel the need to let you know what's happening with your son and with Steven. I was hoping it wouldn't come to this, that our relationship would improve with therapy, but it hasn't. To be honest, we went to two sessions before he refused to go back. He's been abusive towards me, towards our cats, and towards your son. When he's over on the weekends, our fights don't stop just because he's staying with us. Even when I beg him not to fight in front of him, he continues. I want you to know that I have tried everything in my power to stop him from being abusive towards us, but I realize now I can't. Two weeks ago, on our way to drop him off at your house, we got into a huge argument in the car driving down I 25. He stopped the car in the middle of the highway, veered over to the side of the road, and kicked me out. He took out your son's car seat with him in it and left us on the side of the road before taking off. I had to call the police, who sent the state patrol, to come to get us. I'm so sorry for not telling you sooner. But there's more. He choked me in front of him, and when your son started crying, he stopped. I called the cops, which is why we weren't there the night you came to pick him up, and he was at his grandmother's house. I'm more worried about your son than myself anymore. I need you to know he's in danger, and I'm too scared to call the cops on him. I've called them several times before, and it only makes things worse. I'm too afraid to call you, so this letter is the only way I know how to tell you of the horrible things Steven has been doing to us. He's already killed the cat. Who's going to be next?

Get your son away from him.

Heather

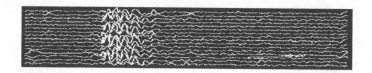

How do you feel as the asphalt under your car seat attracts the sun above your head?

As the cars whoosh by, so familiar, like cartoons on Saturday mornings. You feel the earth underneath you shake. Time slows and blurs around you. It's like I always tell you, ssshhh, sweet boy, everything will be alright.

Now, you are protected, still buckled in your car seat. A woman is running towards you with red pleather shoes and blonde hair. The wind is rising, and sand from the side of the highway blowing in your eyes. Horses and cows dot the horizon, and their necks bend in lazy duty.

A stuffed crocodile we named Burt falls from the car door when he leaves you on the side of the highway. What is the difference between a crocodile and an alligator? Hold your body stiff against the wind. Babies are so resilient. You do not avert your eyes from him when he yells in your face. When he throws you from the car in the middle of a busy highway.

In my dreams, you were never there.

You've fallen asleep on my chest again, smelling of my milk and Lavender powder.

He Was Always Mine

...Parents who kill their offspring in a deliberate attempt to make their spouses suffer. The prototype is found in Euripides' play, Medea. After killing their two sons, Medea told her unfaithful husband, Jason, "Thy sons are dead and gone. That will stab thy heart" (Oates and O'Neill, 1938). The most common precipitants for spouse revenge filicide are spousal infidelity and child custody disputes[xvi].

"Your son tried to choke another child today."

It was early fall in Denver. Me, you, and Alex had been living together for two years. Your father married Heather, and they were still living in The Springs. We had a verbal agreement that you were to stay with him every other weekend, which was a huge hassle for me since I was the one who had to drive you down Friday nights after

---

[xvi] Filicide in the United States
  https://www.ncbi.nlm.nih.gov/pmc/articles/PMC5282617/

work when he returned you to me on a leisurely Sunday drive. You were enrolled in full-day preschool while working at a local finance center as a bankruptcy collections investigator. Alex was working as a loan officer, dreams of pursuing an MFA were still on the horizon, knowing he couldn't leave us to go out of state because of my custody agreement with your father or risk a long-distance relationship.

Our cat Pete had been missing for two weeks, a cat Alex and I adopted from the shelter a year earlier. We had a special bond. My dreams were filled with him running down the sidewalk in front of our house, just out of my reach, an orange and white blur always leaving, returning, but never staying. It was a Thursday, and I was getting ready to leave for work later than usual when your preschool called me.

"Your son tried to choke another child today." The preschool director, Mary, told me, and I felt the instant weight of fear drop into my gut.

"Are they alright? What happened?" I felt a tornado of fear tearing its way up from my guts into my throat.

"She's fine. There was no damage, no bruising. To be honest, it was more of a mimic he was doing as if he were imitating someone. When I asked your son why he did it, he told me his dad had done the same thing to him." There was a pause, and I heard children screaming and laughing in the background. The noise began to mix together until I could no longer tell the difference. "Ms. Leftwich, if I'm being candid here, your son has never been an issue until recently. His behavior has completely changed. Is the father living with you, if you don't mind me asking?"

There are moments in life when a bomb drops, and you don't remember much of the explosion, only the aftermath. This was one of those times. I remember leaving work and driving during rush hour to pick you up from school. I remember the looks the staff members at the preschool gave me as I brought you out with me. Mary assured me that you were not getting removed from their program if I could provide proof of a report made to Child Protective Services, which I did the next morning. I remember taking you home and making you dinner; barbeque beans, chicken strips, chocolate pudding, then telling Alex what happened. I remember dialing your father's number and him answering, the noise from the bar he worked at filling my ears, a mixture of drunken laughter and pool sticks hitting balls, the clinking of beer mugs. I remember yelling so loud that I'm sure the neighbors five blocks down heard me as I told your father he was no longer allowed to see you. He would never see you again, and that was a promise, not a threat. I was hiring an attorney and would be suing him for full custody. I remember my voice going hoarse the next day, and I barely recognized myself. In a matter of moments, I went from someone I thought I knew to someone else. This other person was on the fucking war path, and she had completely taken over.

"You'll never see my son again," I told him. "He's mine. He was always mine." That night, Pete returned home to me, looking the same as he had when he left.

That night, your seizures came back full force, and they were unstoppable.

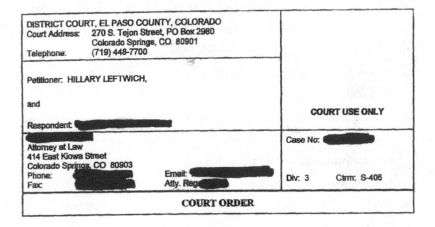

DISTRICT COURT, EL PASO COUNTY, COLORADO Court Address: 270 S. Tejon Street, PO Box 2980 Colorado Springs, CO. 80901 Telephone: (719) 448-7700	
Petitioner: HILLARY LEFTWICH, and Respondent: █████████████████	**COURT USE ONLY**
████████ Attorney at Law 414 East Kiowa Street Colorado Springs, CO 80903 Phone: ████████████ Email: ████ Fax: Atty. Reg ████	Case No: ████████ Div: 3 Ctrm: S-406
COURT ORDER	

THIS MATTER came before the Court July 2, 2009, for hearing upon parenting time, parental decision-making, child support, and name change for the child. Petitioner/Mother, HILLARY LEFTWICH, appeared by counsel, ████████████████████ Respondent/Father appeared in person without counsel. The Court having received the evidence and reviewed its file and now being duly advised in the premises does hereby FIND AND CONCLUDE AS FOLLOWS.

1. The Father of the minor child, ██████████████, date of birth, February 20, 2004 has committed domestic violence repeatedly, both verbal and physical against Mother and a previous spouse in the presence of the child and over a substantial period of time. It appears Father has also choked the child on one occasion.

2. Thus, unsupervised parenting time by Father would endanger the child's physical health and significantly impair the child's emotional development.

3. The parenting plan stated below serves the best interests of the minor child.

4. Father is able-bodied, recently employed, and is imputed a gross monthly income as $1,773.00 per month. The child's portion of health insurance paid by Mother is $77.00. Mother's daycare required for employment is $630.00 per month. Her gross income is $3,905.00 per month.

5. The child suffers from epilepsy and is being treated by a pediatric neurologist at Denver Children's Hospital. The child was hospitalized for five days in mid-June for treatment and evaluation of the recent onset of cluster seizures. The child is presently prescribed four different medications for the epilepsy. The dosage of three may require adjustment from week to week after

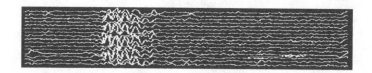

There was a space when the world and everything in it was still mine, not his. A moment before he took everything from me. It was open, raw, a deep cut from past traumas, but it was mine.

Once, when I was seven or eight years old, I stood in a field of wildflowers while hiking up trails for what seemed like miles with my mother, father, and older brother. They disappeared into the woods as I veered away from them, drawn to the explosions of yellow, red, blue, and purple wildflowers rocking in the breeze. I was mesmerized, examining each tiny petal, my small fingers rubbing what felt like old silk between my thumb and forefinger. My parents and brother were gone. No one knew where I was. I was the only one left in a small world full of flowers that stretched to the sky.

You can have my memory because all of yours have been erased.

Songs of Survival

The bedroom was almost packed, leaving bare walls and a hollowness that felt like bird bones scattered to the winds. The mattress frame dismantled and folded, a praying mantis ready to open its body and suck me back inside, leaned in the corner by the window. The box spring and mattress were naked save for a small woven blanket and two stained pillows without their cases, unable to hide the years that would never be washed away. The sun was halfway through a descent into night, catching the small room on fire with an orange haze too bright to be anything but another pollution pallet color to marvel at. And you, lying on the floor between the mattress and the closet in your Scooby-Doo pajamas, feet splayed apart, balled fists at your side, neck stretched and throat exposed, eyes rolled into the back of your head. A poster child for *seizure*. I checked the time on my phone, 5:43, and smoothed your hair as I always do, *ssh, ssh*; not sure if you could hear me. When doctors say they don't know everything about the brain's mysteries, maybe this meant you could. Hear me. Time moved as if drowning in syrup as my phone showcased 5:53. Ten minutes had passed. Ten minutes and your seizure refused to stop. Time to go.

We bought McDonald's. We never bought McDonald's. Still, the food was packed and the refrigerator already emptied; our half-empty burger wrappers flapped as if given wings in the breeze of the ceiling fan. Before, there were routines in place; bedtime stories filled with sleepy smells of lavender bath wash and my words bouncing through the air of your room as they gave birth to terrible neon dragons breathing flames of purple and pink. Your face scrunched in concern as I told you dragons weren't real, monsters especially, but I knew it was a lie. Mothers don't lie unless it's meant to protect our children, and even then, it's a double-edged sword. Your neurologist told me stress brings about seizures, but no one could have warned me of what was to come—a life pregnant with terror and survivor songs that led us to a pattern of running, always running.

Fear sunk into the slow, calculated world of seconds and minutes. I picked you up again into my arms and ran down the set of stairs leading to the parking lot, set you inside of the car, and drove you back, even though we just left the sterilized ER with its cutting, crisp noises, and sharp smells. Even though they said you were stable. And I had grown tired of words that spoke of comfort and grounding when they were as thin as the air in the hospital hallways. And I knew about careless words. We had lived lifetimes of them. Scooby-Doo pajamas looked out of place in a hospital, but then again, so did children. The wires were hooked up to your head once again, and the waves of electricity from your poor, tired brain showed themselves as angry black waves on the computer above your hospital bed. And I could do nothing else with time or protective lies. And I could no longer run. Instead, I sang our songs of survival as the waves of electricity continued to rise and fall.

TCH MAIN CAMPUS
13123 East 16th Ave. B150
AURORA, CO 80045
IP Encounter Report

LEFTWICH,

DOB: 02/20/2004, Sex: M
Adm: 03/21/2008, D/C: 03/21/2008

ED Notes - All Notes

ED Notes signed by Plesich, Mary Jo M. at 03/21/08 0657

Author:	Plesich, Mary Jo M.	Service:	Emergency	Author Type:	Registered Nurse
Filed:	03/21/08 0657	Note Time:	03/21/08 0648		

Pt arrived alert active with parents. Mom stated that pt had a seizure in 2002 where he needed to be rescusitated. For 3 months mom stated pt has had staring spells in school annd then throws up. Pt has seen his pmd and the PMD told mom he thought he had a virus. Tonight Dad stated that pt was staring and eye were fluttering. Pt was standing and was incontinent. Then he was disoriented and shaking for about 10 minutes. Pt was not able to speak or focus.pt arrived alert and able to ambulate.pt appears pale and is still disoriented. Pupils are PERRLA. Lungs are clear. Pt is congested. Has a history of a cold for a few days per mom.pt c/o he has to poop and is gagging and has nausea in triage. Pt did start to shake his arms and legs for a few seconds but was not staring. Mom carried pt back to a room with an RN.

ED Notes signed by Plesich, Mary Jo M. at 03/21/08 0701

Author:	Plesich, Mary Jo M.	Service:	Emergency	Author Type:	Registered Nurse
Filed:	03/21/08 0701	Note Time:	03/21/08 0700		

Pt has had no fever . With the last seizure pt had a full neurology workup and did not have a fever then either per mom.

ED Notes signed by Miller, Sara E. at 03/21/08 0716

Author:	Miller, Sara E.	Service:	Emergency	Author Type:	Registered Nurse
Filed:	03/21/08 0716	Note Time:	03/21/08 0713		

0700 Agree with triage assessment. MOC at the bedside, informed of care by RN. Identifier checked by RN and verified. PT placed on CR monitor & pulse ox. Bedrail up and covered with blankets as seizure precaution. MOC oriented to room, call light and instructed to have bed rail up at all times for safety. Instructed to notify RN if seizure occurs. Pt comfortable. Jitters are resolving.

ED Notes signed by Miller, Sara E. at 03/21/08 0848

Author:	Miller, Sara E.	Service:	Emergency	Author Type:	Registered Nurse
Filed:	03/21/08 0848	Note Time:	03/21/08 0848		

0845 PT remains sleeping at this time

ED Notes signed by Miller, Sara E. at 03/21/08 1008

Author:	Miller, Sara E.	Service:	Emergency	Author Type:	Registered Nurse
Filed:	03/21/08 1008	Note Time:	03/21/08 1008		

1015 PT awake & talking. AAAOx3 MAEW. No jitters not at this time. PT appropriate for age. PT currently watching TC and eating a popsicle.

ED Notes signed by Miller, Sara E. at 03/21/08 1037

Author:	Miller, Sara E.	Service:	Emergency	Author Type:	Registered Nurse
Filed:	03/21/08 1037	Note Time:	03/21/08 1036		

1035 Pt discharged home by emergency room provider, Lundgre, MD. MOC states she has no further questions. Pt is awake & appropriate. PT has tolerated 1 popsicle & a bowl of cereal at this time. No further seizure activity noted

ED Notes signed by Lundgren, Ingrid S. at 03/21/08 1059

Author:	Lundgren, Ingrid S.	Service:	Emergency	Author Type:	Physician
Filed:	03/21/08 1059	Note Time:	03/21/08 0727		

CC: Shaking
HPI: ⬛⬛⬛ is a 4 year old male who arrived to the ED via private car for concern of seizures. ⬛⬛⬛ has had 1 seizure today. The episode occurred this morning. Patient slept well last night. This morning he woke up as usual to get ready for school. Parents were also awake and noticed that he seemed very quiet. Mom's partner found ⬛⬛⬛ standing in the kitchen holding the cat food cup to feed the cat. He was standing in one place, had wet his pants, his right hand, holding the cup, was shaking and his eyes were moving back and forth. Eyelids were not fluttering. Mom's partner tried to remove the cup from his hand, but he was gripping it so tightly that he had to pry it out. He did not respond to voice. Seemed to be breathing normally and was not pale or cyanotic. They estimate that this lasted between 3-5 minutes. Afterwards, he was trying to talk, but it was incomprehensible for about 30 minutes afterwards. He seemed sluggish and was kicking his leg (they think the left, but can't remember) He seemed sleepy on arrival here and finally was able to say "mom". In triage he felt the need to have a bowel movement urgently and was not incontinent. Prior to arrival, the patient received no medications. After the epsidoe ⬛⬛⬛ was sleepy for 30 minutes. ⬛⬛⬛ has not had a fever. He has not had a stiff neck.

ROS: Mother reports a history of no other contributory symptoms and cold symptoms - cough and rhinorrhea for a few days. He has h/o otitis media - last AOM was over 3 months ago. Complete ROS reveals no other contributory findings.

Page 3

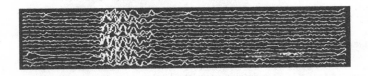

au·ra

Alternative–paranormal

A subtle energy field which is believed to envelop the human body and correspond to the soul.

"The idea that epilepsy is a supernatural, demonic or spiritual disorder persisted with widespread beliefs that it was due to possession by the devil, a notion which obtained support from the miracle story of the cure of the epileptic child recorded in three Gospels. Epilepsy was also viewed as a result of a person perpetrating evil doings, or as a consequence of cycles of the moon or mystic magical phenomenon. Although Hippocrates (c. 400 BC) and his followers regarded it as a physical disorder due to natural causes, only in the 19th and 20th centuries have rational and scientific notions replaced primitive concepts of the medical Dark Age. Galen of Pergamon (AD 130–200) performed no autopsies but described three types of fits and deduced that epilepsy was a brain disorder related to an accumulation of thick humours. Galen says the moon governs the periods of epileptic cases; hence, Greeks and Romans often regarded them as lunatics[xvii]."

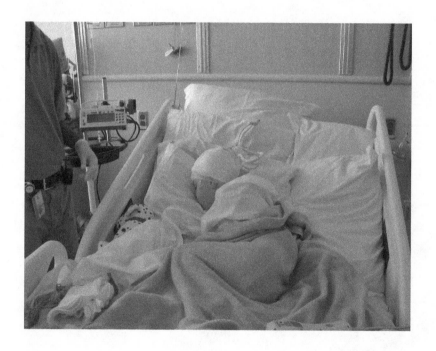

[xvii] A Disease Once Sacred. A History of the Medical Understanding of Epilepsy: J. M. S. Pierce. *https://academic.oup.com/brain/article/125/2/441/297016*

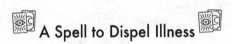 A Spell to Dispel Illness

Write the following on a piece of paper:

ABRACADABRA

ABRACADABR

ABRACADAB

ABRACADA

ABRACAD

ABRACA

ABRAC

ABRA

ABR

AB

A

Fold three times away from you, so the letters don't show. Carry close to your chest or place close to the person who is sick. When the illness is over, bury the paper off your property.

Bury the sickness like a body left to rot.

Bury the sickness with the same care and love of the deceased, so it might rest.

Bury the sickness and never look back.

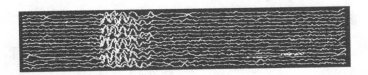

Red

The stripes painted on the walls of the ER. I hold you as you seize and wet yourself. You are five years old. The nurse grabs you from me and takes you to the back, away from the eyes of the people in the waiting room. The seizure lasts about a minute, enough time to type out a text, smear on lipstick, or heat up a slice of leftover pizza and watch the pepperoni's edges curl. Enough time to cause permanent brain damage and death.

Green

The EEG wires taped to your head. The same shade of green the sky holds itself to before a tornado tore through my neighborhood when I was six. The storm killed two of our neighbors, their dog, and destroyed almost all the neighbor's houses. Except ours.

The neurologists order you to wear an EEG cap day and night to record your seizures. The nurse hands me a controller with one green button on it. She tells me to push the button anytime I see you having a seizure. The computer records the point in time on your brainwave chart when the button is pushed. She tells me I cannot sleep. She tells me I have to stay awake to push the button. This is my job now. Push the button. It has become a mantra: *Push the button, push the button, push the button.*

White

The bleached sheets on your bed. It is the second day, and I have not let go of the controller except to go to the bathroom. I push the button and lose count at fifty. I take a moment to stare at myself in the mirror. The fluorescent lights showcase the black clouds under my eyes, pimples, two-day-old makeup, and permanent ponytail. The neurologist in charge of you is a young brunette about nine months pregnant. She exudes all the grace and glow I lack. She tells me they are unable to control your seizures. I wonder if she fears for her own baby's life. If the thought ever crosses her mind that epilepsy might be contagious. You are unconscious. The doctors have you on three different intravenous medications. I am stone now. Unbreakable. I nod my head and watch the words move her lips. I hear the sound of crying from the hallway of the children's ward. It is an eerie, desperate wail. The sound of a mother who will have to bury her child. The sound of the mountain lions roaming the neighborhood around my dad's house, prowling, and hunting. I remember when one of them killed our cat Sheeba one night after escaping out the back door. The next morning, we found her body torn apart, nothing left but a black tail and four limbs.

Yellow

The haze outside the hospital window. The color of your IV medication, a swollen liquid liver wrapped in durable plastic. I poke at it, remembering that I found a fat lemon drop-colored caterpillar on the sidewalk outside my father's apartment as a little girl. My fingernail pierced its squirming body, and a green paste oozed from the soft underbelly. I watched as it curled into a fetal position and did not move.

Day three comes, and the neurologists are unable to stop the seizures. They administer a fourth medication because why the fuck not? Everything feels like a crapshoot now. They tell me I no longer need to push the button and take my controller away. I feel like I am being punished. I did not push the button quick enough, and now my son is going to die. I lie on your hospital bed next to you. You are a mummy wrapped in head gauze and hospital sheets. I touch your cheek and remember when you were soft and perfect. You are unrecognizable to me now. I fixate on the television across from the bed. Oprah talks to me on the screen. She tells me that I get a prize. She points to the audience and tells them they get a prize. She points to the camera and says *to hell with it, everyone gets a prize!* I am elated[xviii].

[xviii] *Their gifts were worth about $13,000 and included a $2,249 TV set, a $2,000 laptop, a $2,189 washer/dryer, sets of $38 champagne glasses and a $495 leather duffel bag. This time, the show's producers had learned their lesson: they also gave each audience member a check for $2,500, which they hoped would cover the tax bill for all the loot. Unfortunately, it didn't quite–most people in the audience owed the Internal Revenue Service between $4,500 and $6,000–but the PR gimmick worked: Oprah's giveaways earned some of the highest ratings in the program's history. Oprah Gives Away Almost 300 Cars: *www.history.com*

Brown

The coffee inside the foam cup. The color of my vomit. Coffee is not a food source. The graveyard shift nurse with the big breasts stomps into the room and starts to shake you. I ask her what the hell is she doing, and she tells me your ammonia levels are too high and you are not waking up. She orders me out of the bed. Get you up, or she will be forced to do a sternum rub. I blink at her, trying to process. She points to the hallway and demands I walk you up and down until you open your eyes. The parents in the other rooms stare at me as I drag you up and down the hallway in my arms, the IV trailing behind us like a loyal dog. There is nothing but waiting and monitors beeping death on this floor. I begin to panic, maybe the graveyard shift nurse hates me and gave my son the wrong medicine, and now your heart is going to stop in the middle of the hallway. I carry you back to your bed, your eyes still shut. I failed again. The nurse says nothing to me as she comes into our room and pushes a chocolate-colored fluid from a syringe into your IV bag. The liquid swirls, tiny and violent. You open your eyes.

Blue

The last good vein in your body. All the other veins have given up and collapsed. Five nurses enter your room and tell me to hold you down. You have been awake for less than an hour, and I am worried you will fall back to sleep. The nurses surround you as if to perform some ancient ritual. I look at the ceiling, out the window, in the hallway, hoping to see something holy. Maybe a glimpse of Mother Mary. Or the ghost of my grandmother, rosary beads binding her hands, her lips moving in prayer like a swarm of bees. I remember you were never baptized. But I do not believe in all of that, heaven or hell. I do not believe in anything anymore. They push a needle into your ankle vein, and you buck, screaming so loud my ears hum, and all I hear is the rush of blood in my own veins. I push more of my weight down, watch as your face contorts, eyes pleading for me to stop. I push harder until the IV is in place. The nurses scatter like birds to the sky, and I am left alone again.

Gray

A chunk of your hair turns gray overnight, and now you are an old man. My old man son. I touch the strands. Something that normally takes fifty years happened in one night. I can see the crows circling like ghosts on a death watch in the alleyway outside the window. The neurology team enters. I am still pondering your gray when they tell me they still cannot stop your seizures. I have heard this a million times now, and I want to punch them in their throats. Instead, I ask them what this means now. Inducing a coma will be our last hope, they say. They say "our" like you are their son too. They tell me this may mean you will never wake up. A living, breathing statue of a son. I remember a movie I watched with ancient Greek gods and demons battling to the death. There was a monster that was part snake, part woman. She turned men into stone statues with a simple stare. I am not a mother anymore. I am Medusa.

Black

The rectangle hanging on the wall pretending to be a window. The color of the storm inside your brain. My mourning. It is Coma Day.

But you are awake again. I think it is a joke or a hallucination, my mind dying, so I call out for a nurse. She checks your vitals and pages the neurologists. They gather in the room, smiles stretching their lips. With a combination of four different medications, they were able to stop the seizures. They tell me this never happens. They tell me inducing a coma is always the final outcome. They never see a child live through over three hundred seizures in five days. Your EEG charts confirm the seizures have stopped their rampage. One of the neurologists holds up a long piece of paper with ink-waves washing across the page. They are short and smooth. They tell me they will not know the extent of the damage to your brain for days, maybe longer. They will not know if you will be able to walk or talk. You start to stir and reach out for me. I curl my body around yours, rubbing the strands of your gray between my fingers. This is the price you pay for surviving.

The rectangle on the wall frames a red sun rising.

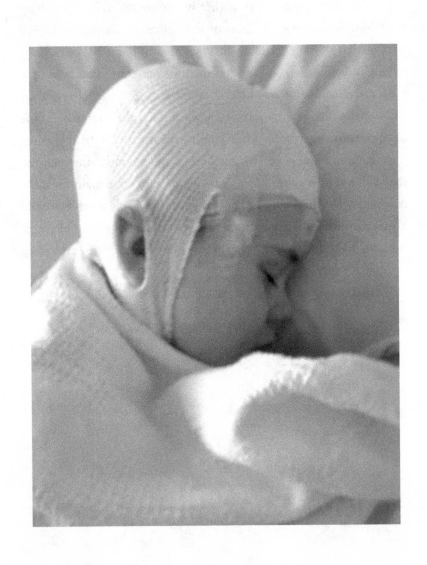

Attorney at Law

March 27, 2009

Mr. ■■■■■■■■■■

Colorado Springs, CO 80918

Re: Post-Decree Matters
        Parenting Time and Relocation Issues

Dear Mr. ■■■■

By way of introduction, Ms. Leftwich has retained me as her attorney concerning her plan to relocate to New Jersey and change ■■■■■ parenting time with you. We believe her plans for ■■■ and herself serve ■■■■ best interests, as is required by law. Please see your required copy of her legal motion enclosed.

The motion, of course, is stated in general terms as required by court rules. We will be consulting you further about Hillary's reasons and concerns in detail.

Please do understand that this legal action is in no way intended as some sort of revenge against you. As a parent, Hillary in good faith believes that these proposed changes in ■■■■ legal rights to parenting time with you are necessary for his health and safety. I have encouraged Hillary to discuss these matters with you in a calm and respectful fashion as the Court expects of good parents. Therefore, we certainly request the same of you. In view of the difficult and perhaps highly emotional circumstances, we ask you to consider communicating with Hillary by letter, rather than some sort of heated phone call or other contact.

Meanwhile, we welcome any contact you may request from the child's present therapist (Dr. ■■■■■■ Psy.D., telephone ■■■■■■ and neurologist (Dr. ■■■■■■, M.D., Children's Hospital Neurology Dept., telephone ■■■■■■.

Yours truly,

Lawrence K. Dean

LKD/pjt
Enclosure

cc: Ms. Hillary Leftwich

Well, You Know, You Just Have to Hang in There

A fragile woman is known as a scared, timid thing. A *poor thing*. A woman who cannot stand up for herself, who wilts at the mention of anything she feels she can't withstand. I was this wilted woman, this limp, lifeless thing no one wanted to deal with. A sigh and toss into the garbage can.

While you were in the hospital, I struggled to finish my final school semester. I was set to graduate in the summer with a BA in English, but I had to pass my classes, and they wouldn't be offered again until the following year if I dropped them.

I sat next to your hospital bed, Alex's laptop propped in front of me, typing out my final assignments while you slept next to me. There was nothing to be done. Every medication had been given, and every test had been run. I needed something else to focus on, or I would lose my mind. Alex had to work full time and came in the evening to spend time with us, showering at home before heading to work again in the morning. We were in the process of moving into a new apartment. Boxes stacked, food packed away. Alex would be moving back to New Jersey for his MFA at Rutgers, and I would be living alone for the first time since my early twenties.

During this time, the stress of both the court trial and your seizures took a toll on my relationship with Alex, though it wouldn't show until months later. I hung sprigs of angelica and lavender over your bed, taped to the metal framing for protection, mouthed words of protection, drew invisible sigils on your palms with the tips of my fingers, but nothing seemed to help. You weren't getting any better, and no amount of magick or manifestations were going to save you. Maybe the Spirit World knew something I didn't want to admit. I saw shadow people brushing past your doorway at night, sitting in the corners of your room, quick glimpses as they slid past your hospital bed. They were there, waiting. I couldn't fight them. Not while I was still firmly within the Land of the Living, and you were halfway between their world and ours.

The nurses came in shifts, and I knew every one of their names, despite the chaos of our daily life. Lucy came in the early evening, allowing me a moment to step outside and walk down to Colfax to smoke. The hospital was built on a campus with three other hospitals, and it was strictly a non-smoking campus. My friend Nicky, a woman I met while working at Ford Credit, was the only person I felt I could trust to confide in. Her younger niece and sister would hang out frequently at their house and have known you since you were a toddler. I called her number as the cars sped by on Colfax Avenue, cradling my phone against my ear while I lit a cigarette.

"Hey, you. How's he doing?" She asked from the other end of the phone. Her voice sounded strained as if she were reading from a script. I sighed.

"He's sleeping still, barely waking up anymore. Yesterday, we had a real hard time. His ammonia levels were too high, and I had to get him up out of bed and walk him around the hallways. It was so fucked up, Nicky. I felt terrible, everyone staring at me like I was torturing my kid, you know?" Silence on the other end. I took another drag off my cigarette, needing the nicotine to flood over my body, needing anything to take the place of the fear eating its way through me. She finally cleared her throat.

"Well, you know, you just have to hang in there and try to stay strong as best you can." I flicked the ashes from my cigarette and watched as one of the homeless men standing near the bus stop shelter ran into traffic while there was a red light. He stopped and bent down to look at something in the middle of the road. I wanted to punch her through the phone. I wanted her to feel the anger and hurt I was feeling.

"I know. I'm trying to. But it's tough. Alex still has to work, we're trying to move, my dad and stepmom are down in The Springs, and my mom has to work too. It's just me here alone with him." There was a sigh on the other end of the line. "Do you think you could stop by soon? You mentioned a few days ago that you might be able to, and I could use someone to talk to other than the night nurses. They're tired of hearing me talk." I forced a laugh in an attempt to make light of the situation, but there was no making light of the situation. Not then, not now. I was losing my mind, and I needed a friend.

"I don't know. I have to help my sister with Rachel's birthday party. She's turning six, you know. And I'm slammed at work. I'll try, okay? Just hang in there. I'll talk to you soon." The line was dead before I had the chance to respond. No one wanted to be around me. It was as if I had a disease, and they didn't want to catch whatever was making my life hell. My blood was pooling too close to their own feet. I knew the burden of it all was too heavy for me to carry, let alone expect to have someone else hold for me. Still, I couldn't help but feel a tiny ball of solid fear and anger forming in my guts, rising up until I felt like I was floating.

Not only was I living at the hospital with you, not knowing if you were going to live or die, but I was having to fight for custody and traveling from Denver to the Springs to meet with a lawyer I couldn't afford. Your father decided it would be a good idea to represent himself, which my lawyer thought was hilarious, and the trial took place the next day. Alex would stay with you while I was gone. I did not tell your father anything about your hospitalization. He didn't deserve the right to know. He had done this to you. As far as I was concerned, he could die, never knowing or seeing you again.

The homeless man in the street found his treasure. He picked up a quarter and held it in the air, staring at it as if he were holding the moon between his thumb and index finger. I silently cheered for him. The light changed to green, and cars started coming his way. He startled, realizing where he was again, standing in the middle of Colfax, and began to run towards the sidewalk, holding his quarter in front of him as if it were telling him exactly where to go.

A Spell to Influence

I write the full name of the family court judge on a torn lunch sack I take from the hospital cafeteria. I write my name on top of his. I take a nail I found around the construction site outside the main hospital building and tie it with a red thread I unraveled off one of my flannel shirts. I walk as far away as I can from the hospital, going north up Colfax where there are still abandoned sections and fields, drive the nail into the ground with my palm and watch as the earth caves around it. I conjure Our Lady of Sorrows in my mind and whisper a prayer to motherhood, to all mothers, that our children will be protected. That we will be forgiven for trusting in those who made promises to protect us but inflicted only pain and suffering.

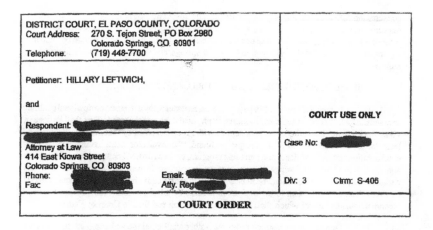

DISTRICT COURT, EL PASO COUNTY, COLORADO
Court Address: 270 S. Tejon Street, PO Box 2980
Colorado Springs, CO. 80901
Telephone: (719) 448-7700

Petitioner: HILLARY LEFTWICH,

and

Respondent: ███████████

COURT USE ONLY

Attorney at Law
414 East Kiowa Street
Colorado Springs, CO 80903
Phone: ███████ Email: ██████████
Fax: ███████ Atty. Reg: ████████

Case No: ████████

Div: 3   Ctrm: S-406

COURT ORDER

THIS MATTER came before the Court July 2, 2009, for hearing upon parenting time, parental decision-making, child support, and name change for the child. Petitioner/Mother, HILLARY LEFTWICH, appeared by counsel, ██████████████████ Respondent/Father appeared in person without counsel. The Court having received the evidence and reviewed its file and now being duly advised in the premises does hereby FIND AND CONCLUDE AS FOLLOWS:

1.   The Father of the minor child, █████████████, date of birth, February 20, 2004 has committed domestic violence repeatedly, both verbal and physical against Mother and a previous spouse in the presence of the child and over a substantial period of time. It appears Father has also choked the child on one occasion.

2.   Thus, unsupervised parenting time by Father would endanger the child's physical health and significantly impair the child's emotional development.

3.   The parenting plan stated below serves the best interests of the minor child.

4.   Father is able-bodied, recently employed, and is imputed a gross monthly income as $1,773.00 per month. The child's portion of health insurance paid by Mother is $77.00. Mother's daycare required for employment is $630.00 per month. Her gross income is $3,905.00 per month.

5.   The child suffers from epilepsy and is being treated by a pediatric neurologist at Denver Children's Hospital. The child was hospitalized for five days in mid-June for treatment and evaluation of the recent onset of cluster seizures. The child is presently prescribed four different medications for the epilepsy. The dosage of three may require adjustment from week to week after

consultation with the neurologist. Due to the acute and unstable phase of the child's illness the child requires daily monitoring and keeping a behavioral diary by Mother. A fourth medication is also prescribed for emergencies. On these occasions the child's health would be threatened by a round-trip transportation for him from Denver to Colorado Springs, and emergency hospitalization may be required.

IT IS THEREFORE ORDERED, ADJUDGED, AND DECREED:

1. Father shall submit to a psychological assessment by a licensed professional qualified to determine whether he presents an emotional or physical danger to the child. This shall be done by Pikes Peak Mental Health or an independent provider recommended by that facility. Father shall bear the entire cost thereof. If danger is found, the evaluator shall recommend a peer confrontation/domestic violence and parenting program, such as AMEND or a program of like nature and quality in Colorado Springs, if any. Father is required to provide Mother's counsel any necessary releases of information. Mother and counsel specifically shall be granted access directly by Pikes Peak Mental Health to the evaluation process by telephone and mail. Each party shall receive the results thereof which shall be reduced to writing and filed in Court by Father.

2. During this assessment progress, Father shall continue and complete his 17-week parenting class with the parent nurturing program at Family Connections. In the alternative, should Father choose to do so he may terminate parenting classes with Family Connections and substitute the AMEND domestic violence and parenting program and Castle Rock, Colorado (telephone (303) 220-1911).

3. Father shall have supervised parenting time with the child through the Central Visitation Program, 1600 Sherman Street, Denver, Colorado 80203; (telephone (303) 839-8701, fax (303) 813-0920; email: CVPDenver@aol.com). This parenting time shall be for one hour on alternate Fridays in accordance with the internal protocol of that organization. The parenting time should be increased as soon as possible to four hours on alternate Saturdays. The expense of this program shall be divided equally between the parents. Father shall bear his expenses for transportation.

4. Mother shall be the primary residential parent for the minor child.

5. The requested change of the minor child's name requested by Mother is hereby denied.

6. Mother is hereby granted sole parental decision-making with respect to religious training, mental and physical health care, general welfare and extracurricular activities, provided however that she initiate timely, good faith advance consultation with Father. If no agreement can be reached, Mother is then authorized to make the final decision.

7. Judgment is hereby entered against Respondent and in favor of Petitioner for $990.00, representing unpaid child support for the months of April, May, and June, 2009. Commencing July

Kung Fu

Guilt, come to find out, is a rotten ball of putrid stank that every single one of us carries around at some point. We try to get rid of it the easiest and fastest way we can. Sometimes, it never goes away. Sometimes, we just have to sit down and eat what we have created, swallowing every last bit of nasty funk that threatens to weigh us down, drown us even, until eventually, we give in.

Every time I look at our cat Larry, this same putrid stank ball rises up into my throat and chokes me. Larry is a reminder of how I escaped and Heather didn't. The first time I met Larry, I stood in your father's living room watching his cat Sargento tremble and hiss under the kitchen table. Larry was just a kitten—a tiny orange tabby that fit in the crook of my arm. Tabby cats were Steven's favorite. Heather said your father killed Sargento months later and had witnessed him do it (according to the police report). I knew I had to get Larry the fuck out of there. I managed to save him with fifty dollars and a used box set of Nirvana *With the Lights Out*.

Larry wasn't his name yet. He was known as Simon at the time. When I brought then-Simon now Larry home, you ran through a series of names to call him, Pizza Cat, Noodles, Stripe, Orange Head, and Spaghetti. It wasn't until I ditched a Craigslist ad for "Free Kitten to Good Home" that I settled on his new name.

Even though I rescued Larry a week prior with no intention of keeping him for myself, I was opposed to the idea of trusting someone else to care for him. The possibility he might become abused again was too much of a risk. I knew that more than anyone.

During my three-year relationship with your father, I was forced to listen and watch him torture our animals. Sometimes he locked himself inside the bathroom with my cat and an electric shaver. He also threw my dog down the stairs while you stood on the bottom step, and there was the time he choked Swirly, our cat. Knowing they wouldn't fight back, he was practicing on them to build his confidence. It wasn't long into our relationship before he turned his anger on me, and I became one of the animals too. I hid inside closets, behind locked doors, and inside the safety of the car with you in my arms, waiting out his anger. There are times when the guilt of the ghosts of our animals emerges to the surface of my mind so violently that I find myself crying just as hard as I did at the moment.

Survivor's Guilt is a psychological condition some people experience after surviving a life-threatening ordeal. Animals can be known to display aspects of this as well. When I brought him home, Larry didn't show any signs. After I introduced him to my older cat, Pete, If he was sad about the loss of his previous companion, Sargento, he didn't let on. He took to his new roommate immediately, and in turn, Pete showed him the same amount of indifference he did with everyone. As the months went by and Larry transitioned into being part of the family, he became anxious, crying loudly at night, pacing the floor, hiding under the bathroom or kitchen sink counter if a man entered the room, and cowering if I tried to pull him out. Only when we were alone during the quiet hours of the morning or night would Larry appear from his hiding spot, meowing for me and rubbing his face against mine, desperately trying to sit on my lap.

In an episode of *Kung Fu*, young Brown says, "You know what Caine says? Whenever someone saves another's life, he's responsible for him forever." I felt this with all the heaviness of the choices I have made I can't undo. How one decision can't balance out the weight of another.

I wasn't surprised when your father was arrested for assault and battery and cruelty to animals. Heather managed to escape before he could do any more damage after attempting to bite her ear off and choke her until she lost consciousness. It was a reminder of what I had somehow managed to save us from. Still, the guilt laid heavy on me. Heather had been my saving distraction during my failing relationship with Steven during the last month. They worked together and formed a close friendship, and once I saw an opening, a possible escape from the abuse that was escalating, I took it. I knew he was cheating on me, and I turned a blind eye. By the time summer started, your father and Heather were dating, and I was giving him everything I owned and all the money I had for a security deposit on an apartment across town. It was the only way I knew I would stick to getting him to stay away from me and focus on her. She was the sacrificial lamb, the offering to King Kong, the only way I knew I could save us. Heather was beautiful in that all-American-girl kind of way. Heather was smart. Heather was quiet and kind. Heather adopted two kittens named Sargento and Simon. Two years later, when she refused to show up in court for my custody trial and agreed to testify by phone, I pictured her neck, still bruised and swollen, her ear half bitten off from the fury of the man we once shared in separate beds.

I won full custody of you that day and never looked back. But guilt has a way of creeping its way inside of you when you think you've finally moved on. That ball of stank coming back to greet you just when you thought you got rid of it. The only answer is to come closer to the edge, inch your way towards the drop-off and look down, feel the dizziness as you lean towards open space and just admit it. Admit what? The horrific fact that other people will have to suffer to save yourself.

Dear Hillary Leftwich,

Thank you for submitting your Creative Non-fiction. While we are unable to accept "Play Date" for publication, we would like to see more of your work.

Your work was almost there. We liked it but felt it was not quite ready to be forwarded to an editor.

We look forward to reading more of your work.

The Editors

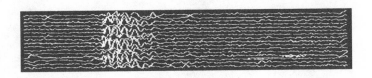

I'm not looking when an old hag creeps into your bedroom. She sits on your chest and steals your breath. Your hair turns gray, and now you are 100 years old. You were a baby once, a long time ago, perfect and soft. Outside, a stray dog is barking at something it cannot see but senses. Its barks turn into growls. You are shaking in your bed. I can hear the springs in your mattress whine and creak.

When I read to you, I point at the dog in the picture. DOG, I tell you. "GOD," you say. I point at our cat. CAT. "TAC," you say. We play games. You are good at Memory. You make all the matches. We play into the night, and then I cook your dinner. In between bites, you tense and shake. Your eyes roll back into your head. I wipe your mouth. Outside, the sun tucks itself under a blanket of black until it disappears.

There is sand in tiny piles guarding your door. I step into the sand, the ocean, and its black waves. You are sitting on your bed, rubbing sand out of your eyes. It scatters from your pajamas and hair. I heard stories about the Sandman when I was a child, how he sprinkled sand in the eyes of children to make them sleep. Once, I woke up and could not open my eyes. Once, I woke up and could not remember who I was.

There are no stars outside your window. The night sits heavy as a giant and the wind sighs, tickling the trees. The music box next to your bed tinkles out a sleepy tune. You sit in front of your bed, gathering sand into turrets and a keep, drawbridge, and moat. I gather sand in my hands. Outside, the stray dog is growing hoarse. His barks scrape from the back of his throat. The air inside the room is thick and warm. You curl both your hands into fists and punch your castle. Sand runs out of your hands and onto the floor. GOD! You shout.

DOB: 02/20/2004, Sex: M
Adm: 06/11/2009, D/C: 06/17/2009

Patient Education

None

END OF REPORT

Reason for Visit
Follow-Up   seizures

Diagnoses
Lennox-Gastaut Syndrome with Tonic Seizures [345.10PF] - Primary

Progress Notes

Author	Status	Last Editor	Updated	Created
Milholland, Jean A.	Signed	Milholland, Jean A.	7/8/2009 1:10 PM	7/8/2009 8:17 AM

████████████ is a 5 year 4 month old male.
Patient presents with:
  Follow-Up
  Seizures
Information source: Mother.
Last seen: 2/18/08. Seen in NMU 6/11/08 for several days.

INTERVAL HISTORY:
Since the NMU visit in early June, they increased ███████ Keppra and decreased his Topamax due to very
bad behavior problems. Mother reports that she has not seen any seizures (#1 below) during the day. Daycare is reporting seizures during nap time. During about a 1.5-2 hour nap, the school reported 3 tonic
seizures, the longest lasting about 12 seconds. Mother has heard a few via the baby monitor while he's
sleeping at night.

Classification: Primarily Generalized.
Onset: 11/01/2006.
Last episode of seizure activity: July 2008
Time of day: During sleep.

Seizure description:
1) Eyes open, straight back, arms clench, jaw clenches, holding breath, making a noise. Does not fall down if
standing.
2) The ones that originally started on 11/1/2006 - Staring spells which last about 10 minutes. Does have
twitching on the right side of his face. Other times, his eyes has horizontal nystagmus. Lethargic afterwards
for an hour or so. None since June 24th, just after an increase in his Keppra. None lately.
3) Blanks out for a second and then throws up. Is lethargic after from 5 min to 1 hour. Was occuring every
day, at least once daily before we increased the Keppra on July 2nd. None lately.

EVALUATIONS:

EEG (6/14/09) - Impression: This is an abnormal electroencephalogram due to frontally predominant spike-
and-wave activity consistent with slow spike-and-wave. In addition, there is paroxysmal fast activity.
Electrographically this would be consistent with Lennox-Gastaut syndrome. Seizures are recorded consisting
of an atypical absence seizures, two tonic seizures, and a generalized tonic-clonic seizure. This represents a
significant improvement from the prior recording. Read by Kelly Knupp.

EEG (6/11/09) - Interpretation: This EEG obtained during wakefulness and sleep is markedly abnormal due to

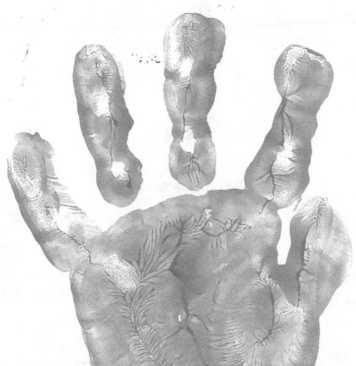

A special handprint that is sure to last,
As my precious little hands are growing so fast.
A sweet memory of when I was small,
As one day soon I will grow to be tall.

Should-Be Mother

Isolation is something that can be felt in the space around you. It's a small emptiness at first, a tiny thing that is inconsequential. But then it grows, feeding off your loneliness until it can no longer be ignored. That's when you know. You're alone and lonely, and you will seek out any kind of human contact to ease the thing that can no longer be ignored. Even if it meant going to the neighborhood fitness club and wearing a string bikini, watching as the married men gawked at you, their wives stuck in the kiddie pools with small, clingy children. Even if it meant driving the 45 minutes into Denver just to grab a drink with a friend to prove you weren't *that* isolated.

It was spring, and we lived alone, you and I, in an apartment on the eastern plains outside of Aurora. Alex had moved back home to New Jersey to finish out his MFA, leaving us deserted in an apartment in the middle of nowhere Colorado. We talked about moving to New Jersey and had plans to move with him, but I changed my mind. I just couldn't see myself relocating while he was attending school. There was too much to consider, too much stress. Alex came to visit during breaks, but the more distance and time spent apart only made the absence in our relationship wider until it was a weight neither one of us could continue to carry. I would wake up in the morning feeling like I was sleeping next to a stranger, our bodies carefully tucked away from each other on opposite ends of the bed.

You were five years old. *The Marvelous Misadventures of Flapjack* played on the TV while you sat on the couch in the living room. One minute you were laughing; we were laughing because Flapjack was hoarding all the candy again. It was a rare moment of happiness after the battle you had gone through at the hospital and recovering. After bringing you home, you were walking and talking backward. It was a strange thing to witness and would have been fascinating had it not terrified me. Not even your neurologists could explain your behavior. They could only assure me it was temporary while your brain rewired itself, like a robot child learning to become human. But the next minute, you were kicking me, punching me with your tiny balled fists, your face red-hot as you screamed. This was how the seizures started since you came home from the hospital with a series of epilepsy medications. I was constantly switching them out, trying to find one that would work, while most of them caused severe side effects such as depression, anxiety, and violent outbursts. You survived the seizures that almost killed you, but the medications meant to save and protect you had turned you into a son I no longer recognized as my own. Was it worse to have a dead son or a son who turned into someone you feared, unable to control?

I found myself avoiding going to grocery stores or anywhere in public with you if I could help it. Once, I took you to the grocery store. Because I didn't give in and let you have a bag of candy that was too expensive for me to afford, you threw yourself on the floor of the aisle and screamed, kicking and punching at nothing, as shoppers slowed down and watched, faces an over-exaggerated mask of startled judgment. I felt their eyes on me, felt them labeling me before I could even react to your tantrum, my face burning with humiliation. I wanted to lash out, a wild animal–just like you were–and tear the looks from their faces with my claws. I was *that* mother with *that* child. Mother monster. Instead, I knelt next to you and calmly asked you to get up, to please listen, but you were having none of it. It was no wonder. You were still being weaned off three different seizure medications and hadn't been sleeping at night. The medications and their psychotic party mix of side effects were wreaking havoc on your behavior and mental state, but the neurologists told me that we had to wait it out until they left your system.

"Please," I begged you, reaching out for your hand to help you off the floor. But you screamed and hit at me, and as a million eyes watched, I picked you up, leaving our cart full of groceries, and walked out of the store as you continued to flail your legs and scream, my entire body burning, a volcano ready to burst. By the time we returned home, you were calm again, as if nothing had happened. Once, I took you to the park to play basketball, something you loved doing. You sat on the edge of the basketball court in the grass, staring off someplace I couldn't see. Just as I was about to ask you if you wanted to play HORSE, you blinked up at me and said,

"Mommy, I want to die."

The Keppra they had you on was notorious for causing depression and other serious mental side effects. But to hear my five-year-old son say he wanted to die was too much to hear, let alone process. I sat down next to you and hugged you as you remained stiff, staring out into an abyss only you could see, my poor baby, my poor baby.

There were storms inside your brain, firing at will, a series of events that began before you were born that sparked this upheaval.

It was never your fault. Still, the set of toddler blows you pounded on my head and stomach that day was too soon, too familiar to your father's fury. As thunder continued to shake the apartment's thin walls, I pushed you off me, crying out as I watched your body hit the wall then fall, a look of confusion and shock transforming your face, feeling a sick hatred for myself, all-consuming, an injured animal. A hot ball of rancid heat and shame. A sick ball of loathing and guilt. You stood up and went into your room as if nothing had happened. I trailed after you, my face was hot with tears, but I wouldn't dare let you see me cry. I needed to be strong, I felt anything less would be failing you, and I had already failed you so many times before. We did our regular bedtime routine–bath time, teeth brushing, and a bedtime story, and neither of us mentioned what happened. I saved my tears for after you were asleep, sinking slowly into my bed as angry, explosive sobs swallowed me until there was nothing left but a shell, yellowed and cracking like a diseased fingernail.

Your neurologists knew it would take time for the medication and its effects to leave your system altogether. Until then, it was a waiting game. They assured me the behavior was due to the drugs and not a result of the damage the seizures had inflicted on your brain. Still, I wondered if this was the truth. They knew nothing, it seemed, always playing guessing games, trying to reassure me with their "the human brain is a mystery" bullshit. I wanted to scream at them that their fancy medical degrees meant nothing if all they could tell me was some euphemistic statement over and over to cover up the fact that they had no clue what was going on with you.

Tell a mother their child is sick but offer no solution. Watch her become a ball of bitterness when she was once a sweet, timid thing.

Later that night, you took a bath and played with your toys, your favorite thing to do. My Pisces baby. Water always calmed you. Water, come to find out, was a savior to us both. It was the only peaceful time I had, a small moment where I could leave the bathroom door open and sit in the doorway, trying to collect my thoughts while keeping an eye on you. One night, my dad called me, and I snuck into the kitchen, still able to see you in the bathtub, and told him about how bad things were, how you were unmanageable, and I didn't know what the hell I was doing. I pulled a Tarot card, and it was The Tower. Of course, it was The Tower. I stared, numb, at the images of people falling from a tall, castle-like structure as black smoke billowed from the windows, bodies in mid-air, a look of horror on their faces. I had become one of them now. Tumbling down into my demise and despair.

"I'm not cut out for this, Dad," I said in a low voice, careful so you wouldn't hear. "I don't know how much longer I can do this. I can't control him."

"You don't have a choice, do you? I'm sorry this is happening to you, but he needs you. You can't give up on him now. You have to keep showing up for him every single day."

I knew he was right, but I wasn't sure how much fight I had left in me. I wasn't sure if I was the right mother for you, a good enough mother, a good enough human to handle all of the issues and battles, and not knowing what the future held for you. I didn't know if you would ever be your sweet self again. Would you continue to be a stranger-son to me? Where did you go?

Should-Be Mother laughed in the corner of the room, the sound of sharp ice cubes rattling in a glass.

You're a terrible mother. And don't blame it on not having any help. Many mothers don't have support and still don't completely lose it.

She sat cross-legged, stacking a tower of multi-colored Legos until they balanced precariously in front of her like a haphazard altar. I wanted to knock her down, tell her she was wrong, that everyone has their breaking point. Everyone is human. I'm a fucking human. But I didn't. I'd had enough confrontation for one night. She stood up and knocked the Lego altar over with her foot as she left my bedroom, glancing back one time with a side smile, tossed her perfectly curled hair away from her shoulders. *I knew Should-Be Mother wasn't real. I knew she wasn't. I knew she wasn't real.*

Somewhere close by, lightning fired across the bruised skies in a series of flash-beats. *One Mississippi, two Mississippi, three Mississippi, four.*

Mourning Period

You were diagnosed with Lennox-Gastaut Syndrome, which can be devastating. Most children diagnosed already have brain disorders such as head injuries, tumors, or brain damage. For the first two days after your diagnosis, I was left wondering if you would develop a brain injury. I checked Google for more information and read stories from parents who had children suffering from Lennox-Gastaut. Many of them were in wheelchairs, would never be able to use the bathroom independently, and were entirely dependent on their parents. One woman posted about a kind of mourning period you go through when your child has severe brain damage or when your child will never be the same again. The realization that they will forever be dependent on you, but they're alive. They will be okay. But they won't be okay in so many ways. Physically, mentally, emotionally. As a parent, you find yourself mourning the child that could have been.

That child's potential—not in an academic or successful sense—but in the sense of being independent of support.

Anyone who's a parent has thought about this at some point. Admit it. But it's never been a concrete reality until the ground slams into you one day, catching you off guard. So I sat on the floor of my upstairs apartment while the cars from Downing Street below sped by. I listened to the laughter of people at the Safeway across the street as they pulled their metal shopping carts from the cart reserve, the wobbling of the wheels aligning with my own shaky heartbeat. They would continue into the store and shop for their everyday food items, not fighting drugged-up, combative toddlers with seizure-damaged brains turning them into monsters. They would buy ingredients for a nice dinner that night, thinking about whether to marinade the chicken in soy sauce and ginger root.

I could hear the school up the block, Dora Moore Elementary, ringing its bell, signaling recess. The sound of the bells hummed inside my head, a vibrational vortex that made me think I might be losing my mind. I vomited all over my lap, the smell of coffee and cigarettes permeating the small room with its one doorway to the outside.

How could I look at you and know you would never be the same again? How could I live with myself knowing I trusted a man to take care of his own son when all he did was hurt you? His violent tendencies exacerbated your seizures, and as a result, you would never be the same child you were before. I was ignorant about your disorder. Your pediatrician and numerous doctors assured me that everything would be fine if they just sent me home with a prescription. There are treatments, but epilepsy will more than likely be a life-long battle for you. I had to learn to be your advocate; it was something I had to go through to become stronger for you.

It took months of switching prescriptions until we found one that didn't cause any terrible side effects and simultaneously controlled your seizures to a point where you only had minor ones at night during your sleep. To go from almost dead to fully functioning again in less than a year was hard to understand, and I'm not sure I ever will. We were lucky, somehow, or maybe we weren't. I knew you would always have problems with memory and other functions and need help in school because of your seizures. I knew life would be more of a struggle than most. No alcohol. No drugs. Even experimenting as a young adult could lead to your death with your epilepsy. Everything comes down to choices. Stupid, brutal decisions. But you're here with me still. Let's be still in this moment together.

Son, there is a storm inside your brain, one that not even the most educated neurologist can stop. It's a storm that may kill you. Living with this fear every day is like living with my own sickness. But life and death can't be manipulated. I know this.

A Spell to Forget Suffering

Capture two small spiders within your home and place them inside of a jar. Tie the lid of the jar with a thick black ribbon or cord. Take the jar to a crossroads and release the spiders, who have always connected the past with the future.

Repeat the following:

I lose you, little spiders, so I will forget about my suffering
I lose you so that you may not find me again
I lose you, so I do not lose myself

TCH MAIN CAMPUS
13123 East 16th Ave. B150
AURORA, CO 80045
IP Encounter Report

DOB: 02/20/2004, Sex: M
Adm: 06/11/2009, D/C: 06/17/2009

Procedures · All Notes (continued)

EEG

Time EEG began: 06/11/09 8:28 p.m. **Time EEG Ended:** 06/12/09 at 6:07 a.m.
Study Number: 09-1426
Study Type:

Reason for Study/Brief Clinical History: [redacted] is a 5-year-old boy with a history of epilepsy which has been intractable to medical treatment. His first seizure was in 2006 and the seizures became more frequent in January 2008. One week ago the patient began having episodes of tensing of his upper extremities lasting up to 15-20 seconds. The number of seizures have been increasing.

Medications: Keppra.

Technical Description: This EEG was performed at the bedside. The 10-20 International system of electrode placement was used, and both bipolar and referential electrode montages were monitored. This EEG was performed during wakefulness and sleep without sedation.

EEG Description: The background EEG activity contained medium voltage 6-7 Hz predominant frequency over the posterior head regions, which is symmetrically in amplitude and reactivity on the two sides.

Frequent nearly continuous 4-5 Hz theta activity was noted in the central vertex and bilateral frontocentral region.

Frequent bursts of generalized 1-2 Hz spike-and-wave discharges with anterior predominance were noted.

In addition, generalized 3-5 Hz spike or polyspike and wave discharges were also noted with anterior predominance intermixed with generalized slow spike-and-wave discharge.

Frequent spike and sharp waves were also seen in the multifocal regions.

Frequent bursts of generalized 2-3 Hz delta activity were noted throughout the recording.

The patient developed 10 generalized tonic-clonic seizures occurring during sleep from 2221 on 06/11/09 to 2331 on 06/11/09. The patient received intervenous Keppra at around midnight. Since then he had no clinical seizures. All seizure were similar and occurred during sleep. He had tonic stiffening of the legs and trunk. The tonic seizures could be either symmetrical or asymmetrical with shifting within both sides. However, it is very difficult to tell as most of the seizures occurred when the patient was lying down on his stomach. The tonic stiffening lasted for approximately 8-12 seconds. After that the patient would be still and start to cry. The EEG 2-3 seconds before the onset of

DOB: 02/20/2004, Sex: M
Adm: 06/11/2009, D/C: 06/17/2009

Procedures - All Notes (continued)

seizures show bilateral auricular sharp waves, which then followed by a generalized spike or polyspike-and-wave discharges, which then were followed immediately by diffuse background attenuation with superimposed very low voltage beta activity. The beta activity then evolved into much higher amplitude up to 200-300 microvolts with the frequency of 15-18 Hz lasting for approximately 4 seconds. After that the EEG showed bilateral synchronous rhythmic 1.5 Hz activity with anterior predominance. The bilateral rhythmic delta activity then evolved into fastest frequency and returned back to the baseline within 45-80 seconds. The seizures were stereotype and compatible with generalized tonic seizures.

During sleep vertex waves and spindles are normal in configuration and distribution. The epileptiform activity mentioned above occurred more frequently during sleep than while the patient was awake.

Hyperventilation and photic stimulation were not performed. After the treatment with intravenous Keppra at around midnight, the patient no longer had clinical seizures.

Interpretation: This EEG obtained during wakefulness and sleep is markedly abnormal due to the following:
1. Slow background activity.
2. Constant theta activity in the central vertex and bilateral frontocentral region.
3. Frequent bursts of generalized slow spike-and-wave discharges intermixed with fast spike-and-wave discharges with anterior predominance.
4. Frequent multifocal epileptiform activity.
5. Ten episodes of nocturnal tonic seizures.

After the treatment with the intravenous Keppra the patient no longer had a seizure.

Clinical Correlation: This EEG is strongly supportive of the diagnosis of CV epileptic encephalopathy. The EEG findings of generalized slow spike-and-wave discharges and generalized tonic seizures raised the possibility Lennox-Gastaut syndrome. However, this in not typical Lennox-Gastaut syndrome in that the background continued to show generalized fast spike-and-wave-discharges. Therefore, clinical correlation is highly recommended.

Pramote Laoprasert, M.D.
Attending Provider

Dictated by: Pramote Laoprasert, M.D.

PL/td
D: 06/12/2009 15:52:18 / T: 06/13/2009 08:15:38
Job ID: 5178560/5178560
Doc#: 4808771 Service:
0

cc:

Dear Hillary,

Thank you for sending us your work about your son and his epilepsy. We enjoyed reading your work. However, it's not the right fit for us at this time, and as such, we've decided to give it a pass.

I'm sorry this isn't a yes—there was a lot to admire here, but in the end, the piece didn't quite come together. Likely another editor will disagree with me, and I wish you luck placing it elsewhere.

We wish you the best of luck placing your piece elsewhere.

Thank you for your interest in our magazine. Please try us again.

All our best,
The Editors

A Good Man

Our lives began to normalize, as well as your seizures—with the right combination of medications—and you started kindergarten. I had a job working remotely from home, and everything seemed peaceful. This was a calm period for us both, a chance to catch our breath after the series of blows we had received. We developed a routine of visiting your grandparents, staying close to home, and resting. You had a few playdates, but since I worked full time, it was hard to attend the parties and get-togethers many of your classmates went to because of my schedule.

Online one day, I came across the local Boy Scouts and decided to take you to the registration event. Drowning in a sea of khaki, I navigated the tables stacked with papers while volunteer scouts sat behind them, busy helping other parents with their questions. I took your hand, led you to a table, and filled out the paperwork, but you were antsy. There were kids from your class there, so I let you go to play in the corner of the room. After about thirty minutes, I turned in the forms. I waited patiently for the information session to begin, taking a seat in the front of the room, feeling awkward when I noticed I was the only person without a partner.

"Ahem," a tall, gangly-looking man patted the microphone placed in the front of the room and cleared his throat. "If everyone can take a seat, we'll begin. There are refreshments provided by our lovely volunteers, so don't forget to stop by the snack table and grab a cookie or two." The room became filled with the noise of people finding their seats until, eventually, the gangly man returned to the mic and began going over the paperwork and the events lined up for the rest of the year.

"We'll be having our annual camping trip in September and encourage fathers to sign up. It's a wonderful opportunity to teach your sons all about survival skills and the joy of camping." I glanced down at my stack of papers and flipped through them, trying to find any information about mother-son opportunities. All I saw were "Father/Son, Father's, Mother's, and Daughter's."

"And so with that, I'll open it up for questions."

"Yes," I blurted, raising my hand. Scout leader pointed at me. "I notice there aren't any activities or opportunities for mothers and sons. Can mothers go on the annual camping trip as well?" Eyes were on me, and I felt completely outed as the only single mother in the room.

"Uh, well, unfortunately not. The annual camping trip is for fathers and sons only. But you're more than welcome to attend any of the fundraising events or learning camps." I felt my face burning and realized I didn't think this boy scout thing through. The questions continued and then stopped after the kids grew restless and started complaining. We returned to our apartment, and I continued searching online for playgroups, meetups, anything to try to find a connection with another parent or parents. But it wasn't easy when most parents, even if divorced, still co-parented. But we were happy with each other, and I took you to as many playgrounds, movies, and school events as I could. And you never complained. Only once did you ask me why we stopped going to boy scouts. When I could only find silence as an answer, you said it was okay.

"Everyone has a daddy but me. I feel sad no one will share their daddy, even just for an hour. They get them all of the time, and I just want a little."

☿

I needed a distraction from the pain, something to keep my mind occupied, and I was empty from the number of losses I had to navigate in a rapid series. Alex and I had finally broken up for good, and I became isolated and lonely. I felt the energy of a trapped wild animal pacing the cage of our apartment like there was no escape. It felt like there wasn't. Even sneaking out on the back deck to overlook the eastern plains gave me no comfort. It was dry, burnt yellow fields leading to nothingness. I was hungry for human touch. Desperate for any kind of contact. I struck up an online relationship with Joseph in a private group for writers on Facebook. There were months of us private messaging each other back and forth until he made his feelings known for me one day.

God, I want you. Is this possible?

I want to marry you.

This is crazy. I have to see you.

I was desperate for any show of affection or love after Alex, so I dropped you off at your grandma's house for the weekend and hopped a plane to Florida, where Joseph lived in Hollywood.

The minute I got off the plane, I knew I had made a mistake, but my heart needed someone, anyone, and Joseph was that anyone. I stopped off in the airport bathroom, staring at myself in the mirror, wondering who the fuck I was anymore. The sound of the overhead speakers announced, "Renee Rodriguez, please meet your party at the gate." I knew I could grab my bag, head to any ticket counter, and catch the first flight home. My family thought I was attending a bachelorette party in Florida for an old college friend, a lie I made up to justify the flight, knowing the entire time I was deceiving my family. For every lie, I had to make up another lie to cover the first lie. But I couldn't go home because I didn't have a home without Alex, even though we lived thousands of miles apart for two years. The hole he left inside me needed to be filled, and I was willing to let anyone take a shovel and start piling on whatever they were offering. I was ashamed, but couldn't face the guilt of my actions, even to myself. Something kept poking me to keep acting on my whims to fill the void that was rapidly spreading. I told myself it could be worse, I could be turning to alcohol or drugs, but it was little reassurance. I spent lifetimes trying to fill voids and holes left by others. The pain of losing Alex and the isolation of my living situation, so far away from Denver and any friends, made me desperate for human contact.

Shame makes you react in reckless ways, Son. We're all just humans trying to live the life we didn't ask to live. One day, you'll know.

☿

From the day Joseph and I met, our sexual appetite was a force. Bearing an uncanny resemblance to Tom Cruise, I almost laughed uncontrollably when I approached him for the first time at the airport, thinking it had to be a joke. He had slightly resembled the actor in his pictures online, but even more so in person. I looked around for hidden cameras, but there were none. Joseph got down on one knee and proposed to me with a candy RingPop while onlookers clapped and smiled. I held my shaking hand out, laughing nervously, as he slipped the ring on my finger. He kissed me hard. almost too hard, our teeth bumping together, causing me to bite down on my lower lip. I was shocked and embarrassed while passersby congratulated us. None of it seemed real. It felt like a scene in an obscure Tom Cruise movie, and I could feel a familiar out-of-body sensation taking over me. As if I were playing my own part in the scene as it unfolded. But it wasn't a scene in a movie. This was my life. And I had chosen to fly across the country to meet a man I had never met in person, who asked me to marry him, and now he was taking me by my hand and leading me to his work truck in the dark underground parking garage of the Miami airport.

He took me through the drive-thru at McDonald's, then drove me to his small apartment in Hollywood, where we ate nervously, barely talking, when he began stripping my clothes off. We woke up nine hours later on his floor, naked and exhausted, sweating in the early morning heat. A month later, Joseph flew to Denver to meet me at my now-empty apartment, all of our belongings given away except for what we needed to take with us in the back of my Jeep. We left Colorado and a home I had hoped to build with Alex behind us, taking three days to drive to Florida with one dog, two cats, and you in the backseat. Florida was a promise of a new home, a new life, and a new husband and father for you. All neatly wrapped in one hastily thrown together package.

We were married on the beach at sunset with Joseph's friends and co-workers. No one was there for me except for you. It was straight out of a Hallmark movie; me in a simple white spaghetti strap gown and Joseph in a black suit and tie, looking even more like some movie star than ever. My long, black hair was curled and blowing in the wind as I stood waiting for the officiant to call me forward. I stared at the waves breaking on the beach, remembering a time when I was ready to move to another side of the country once, ready to commit myself to The Pacific and her ancient energy. How long ago that seemed at the moment. How I felt like an entirely different person standing on another beach, sand invading my heeled sandals, as a man I barely knew smiled at me expectantly, waiting for me to give my life up for him.

I was always giving myself up for men. It never ended. When would I start putting someone other than a man first? When would I be brave enough to put myself first?

It felt right, like I was doing something to better us at the time. But as with most things that start out strong, the strength and resolve eventually begin to taper off. More and more, Joseph demanded sex all of the time. We were matched in our energy and lust for each other initially, but when he never seemed satisfied, I grew more and more exhausted trying to please him. I had forgotten my sex magick, how it was about me just as much as it was about him, and how I wasn't being pleasured at all. It was all about him. What he wanted me to do to him.

I was also experiencing depression again, something that never went away. It continued its grip on me throughout the years. I was worried I wouldn't find work to help support us, and the last thing I wanted to do was give in. But I did. Over and over. Because giving in was easier than standing my ground with a man who refused to listen to reason. Refused to see me except when I was standing naked in front of him, completely vulnerable and exposed.

Joseph never took to you the way he did with his son, which I both understood as a parent and resented him for. You and I moved across the country for him, and he never tried to establish a relationship with you. If I ever thought he would make a good father, it was because he made a promise he would take care of us. The night before we drove from Denver to Florida, we had dinner at my mom's house with my dad, stepmom, and my mom's husband. My dad half confronted, half approached Joseph in the hallway while I spied from the living room doorway, holding my breath. My dad asked him, "You're a veteran, you served in the Army, Joseph, and you seem like a good man. You going to take care of my daughter and my only grandson?" It's a question that Joseph probably anticipated, and he must have had an answer prepared. The kind of response every father wants to hear. He passed the test, and we left the following day with a forced blessing from my parents.

☿

During the day, while you were in school and if I didn't have any job interviews, I would sit by the pool and smoke, calling whoever I could think of to talk to, writing stories I hoped to one day have published in another life that seemed to always escape me. Florida was beautiful if you were in a vacation spot, but it felt hollow and tired where we lived. The people struggled, and no one exerted any effort to be kind. It was a reaction to the survival mode that I knew well. I dialed the number for my sister and lit a cigarette, eyeing the couple drinking Icehouse Lite beers and laughing a little too loudly.

"Hey, what's up?" I asked her after she answered, tapping the end of my cigarette, not taking my eyes off the drunk man lounging at the side of the pool as he crushed another empty can of Lite House against his skull.

"Not much; you okay?" The sound of children yelling in the background fired through the phone like gunshots.

"I guess. Things aren't going too great here, Akira. I'm thinking about coming home." There was a long silence on the other end of the line. Even the kids had stopped their yelling. I tapped my cigarette, a nervous habit. A sigh came through after what seemed like several minutes. I was getting hot, the sun was overhead, and it didn't look like it would rain today. The pool would be crowded again once the kids were released from school.

"I know it's tough, but you have to try to stick it out. I've learned from being married as long as I have that you must keep trying. You can't give up. You know? Things are going to be hard, especially since you just moved there. That's normal. Have you talked to him about all of this?" I took a long drag off my cigarette and watched the smoke curl its way away from me, floating towards the pool.

"I have, and he won't listen to me. I've tried. And every day, it gets worse. His jealousy is terrible. I want to go home." I didn't know what home was, just a state that existed that wasn't Florida. I only knew the summers I spent here as a girl with my grandpa and grandma weren't the same as living here. Florida is a great place to vacation, but not to live.

"Well, just be sure if you leave that you're one hundred percent certain, or you might regret it later. Don't leave any room for regret." I nodded as if she could see me and stubbed my cigarette out on the sidewalk.

I've had enough regret to last into my next lifetime and more. All I wanted, all I still want, is the sound of the ocean and a sense of home.

Hollywood

In 1981 Adam Walsh, the son of John Walsh, was abducted from a Sears in Hollywood, Florida. His head was found two weeks later. The rest of him is still missing.

I thought a lot about Adam Walsh after moving to the same town as him. While you were in school, I chain-smoked and studied Craigslist for jobs. There wasn't shit to do in Florida. The beach was a mile drive down the main road, and I could have easily gone, but you were in school all day, and I didn't want to go by myself. We moved to escape Colorado and my breakup, but the same problems found themselves here.

The Sears where Adam was abducted isn't there anymore, but a Target was. I walked up and down the aisles. I was eight years old when Adam was murdered. I imagined the toy section where he stood twenty-five years prior before he was kidnapped. The Lite-Brites, Battleship, and Monopoly had been replaced with electronic games beeping at me as I looked at the ceiling. A water stain browned cheap white tiles. The closer I stared at it, the more it morphed into a distorted version of the face of Jesus.

There were canals outside of the Vero Beach Airport, and I used Google Maps Earth View before driving to their location. This was the place where two fishermen found Adam Walsh's head. I crouched awkwardly, straining on my ankles. The water was ugly and brown, like the stain on the Target ceiling. Everything in Florida was rundown, exhausted. Even people. They didn't look you in the eye.

The skies were clouding over, and an acrid smell blanketed the air. John Walsh roamed the streets of Hollywood looking for Adam but never found him. He checked every dumpster and back alley, wanting to find something but not wanting to find that something. Adam's mother gorged her guilt with whiskey. Their marriage didn't last. Mine didn't either, for different reasons.

I drove to your school, a dark rectangular building resembling a prison. The students were leaving the doorway in single file lines led by their teachers. I spotted you; a tiny boy weighed down by dark brown curls and a backpack with a monster face stitched on the front. I stuck my hand out my window and waved. You broke from the line and ran, hopping into the car after throwing your backpack onto the back seat. I headed east instead of west, the sun still pinned in the sky, a burning beacon. You asked where we were going, familiar with our usual route home.

"To the beach, baby." You bounced in your seat, eyes wide. Our bare feet stepped on soft sand, and you ran towards the water, a silhouette of someone familiar. You had never seen the ocean, not in person, only from our car window. I wanted to tell you that there was no way of knowing how deep the water was or what creatures lived beneath. I wanted to say that the waves were blue because they reflected the sky, but I stopped myself. Some things shouldn't have an explanation.

Fuck Florida Too

We left Hollywood, Florida, just months after our arrival. Joseph's jealousy and inability to see us as a family rather than singular units—his son, his role as a father, his role with his ex—proved to be too much to untangle. We hit the road in the late afternoon, right before the sun started to settle itself below the horizon. I managed to corral all of the animals in my Jeep; two cats in a large kennel that took up the entire back (the litterbox took up most of the room) and our dog, Frankenweenie, a small spotted Dachshund we bought as a puppy before I met Joseph and after Alex moved back to New Jersey to finish his MFA. He was, as far as puppies go, the cutest chocolate brown, squirming, warm, adoring creature I'd ever had the joy of raising. Between Frankenweenie, my beloved cat Pete, and his sidekick Larry, we were set as far as our animal tribe. The same morning, while going through my usual routine of scanning the online job websites for possibilities while Pete and Larry roamed the nature preserve next to our apartment for prey, Joseph was busy blasting my phone with his usual text messages.

What are you doing now?

I tried calling this morning but you didn't answer.

You know, Chris's girlfriend gets up at 2 am to make his coffee for him before he leaves.

You just lay there in bed.

We're in a remote part of the swamps this week. Check out this gator I spotted while surveying—a picture loads of a six-foot alligator staring through the phone at me with deadpan eyes.

Who are you talking to?

Are you there?

Who are you talking to?

I know you're lonely, but you shouldn't be talking to other men here, even if they're friends. I know how men are.

You there?

You bitch.

Let's fuck tonight when I get home.

You dirty bitch. I'm going to fuck you raw.

Joseph worked as a surveyor for the county and took my Jeep every morning to work, leaving me home alone with no transportation. If I needed the Jeep for a job interview, he would catch a ride with his friend Chris, another surveyor and a part-time drug dealer. His girlfriend, Tammy, was what Joseph called "your typical southern girl" and always woke up with Chris to make him coffee and a hot plate before leaving for work. I didn't. Joseph could take care of himself, and I had you to look after. I wasn't anyone else's mother but yours.

Joseph told me stories whenever he got home from work about his day. He often described the bodies he found in the remote regions of swampland he surveyed. It wasn't uncommon to find corpses where they surveyed land.

"The elements are cruel with the flesh of humans," he said, and by the time he or one of his coworkers found a body that had been dumped, it was hard to tell if it was human at all. The swamplands were a favorite dumping ground for people no one would miss. My heart ached for those souls and their bodies abandoned for the company of ancient lizards and reptiles.

Joseph shared custody of his son, who was four, with his ex-partner Rhianna. She was a licensed psychologist and beautiful, Nordic beautiful, with vivid blue eyes that turned violet in the right light and dark, wavy brown hair. It never got past me that Joseph was still in love with her. A part of me was in love with her too. She was beautiful, smart, and too good for Joseph. I envied her. Their son, Sky, was a smaller version of Rhianna with Joseph's nose and long, lightning-white hair. He looked like a character from Zelda.

Joseph made it easy for me to make my final decision by starting out another morning with another fight. After Chris picked Joseph up for work, leaving me alone with a half-empty apartment, an unpaid utility bill, and a king-sized mattress I used half my savings on with no means to take it with me, what became our final fight was the nail in our relationship's coffin. His jealousy over my feeble attempts to make friends in the area on social media and his inability or lack of wanting to understand how lonely I was at home by myself all day, no one to talk to, searching the craigslist ads for any possibility of a job, was impacting my mental state in ways I was finding hard to deal with. I found myself fixating on the corpses in the swamps, how they got there, particularly the murder of Adam Walsh, John Walsh's son, in the same town we lived in. I knew my headspace was not good, and I needed my mental space to be good for you, or I wasn't doing my job as a mother.

I started packing everything we owned, which wasn't much and throwing it into the same boxes and storage containers we used to move ourselves to Florida. When I was sure I had all of our belongings, I made my way towards your school. It was mid-morning, and that day was Joseph's late workday. I would disenroll you from school and sign the necessary paperwork, telling them we were moving home. That afternoon, I planned to be gone.

As I sat inside your school's front office, waiting for them to get you from class, the paperwork already filled out, I remembered I had promised you we would go to Chuck E Cheese to play some games and grab some pizza. You saw me inside of the office, a look of confusion settling on your face until I smiled and told you we were going to Chuck E Cheese. I figured the best way to tell you we were moving home was on the way there, and I did, a pang of guilt hitting my heart. What was I doing? You had just begun to settle here, and now I was taking you away again. What the fuck was I thinking?

"We're going back home, sweetie," I said, not looking at you in the rearview mirror.

"Going home? To Papa and Mama and Nana?"

"Yes, to all of them. It's time to go home," I said, explaining how home was in Colorado, and we needed to return. We parked and went inside the Chuck E Cheese, and I bought a pile of play coins for you. While you were playing one of the video games, I realized how you were both occupied and unaware of what was happening, how I had moved you from one state across the country to another, only to move back again in less than three months. You only knew we were leaving to go back home and never asked me why. You didn't know Joseph long enough to form a relationship with him, and he never bothered to try with you. I took off my wedding band and twisted it between my fingers. It wasn't worth anything. Joseph didn't make much money, and I was broke, spending my savings on the move. A simple silver band that meant nothing.

After a few minutes, you made your way over to me, asking to go to the bathroom. I took you into the women's restroom with me, not willing to let you be alone in the men's just yet. While you were inside the stall, I stepped into the next empty booth and shut the door behind me, my wedding ring in my hand. I thought of Joseph and Alex. Everything I gave up on moving here, only to turn around and return home with nothing. I didn't know where I belonged anymore. I heard the toilet flush next to me, and you called out, "Mommy! I'm done!" Without hesitation, I dropped my wedding band into the toilet and flushed, watching as it was sucked into the sewer system and taken away from me. The same sewer system the alligators thrived in. Maybe one day, Joseph would come across the ring, somewhere in the swamps of Florida. Maybe he would find it inside the belly of an alligator, slicing the stomach open while the blood-stained his hands, turning the ring over like a treasure he forgot existed.

I heard someone snort outside my bathroom stall, then begin laughing, watching as a shadow formed, knowing it was Should-Be Mother. I didn't care. Fuck her too. I unlocked the hatch on the door and kicked it open, much to the surprise of the other women and their small children washing their hands at the sink inside. I grabbed your hand, and as we walked toward the bathroom door, I flipped my head back and took one last glance at the line of women behind me.

"Fuck Florida too," I shouted, yanking the door open as we made our way towards the exit of Chuck E. Cheese.

I hurried to get all our clothes in my Jeep along with your stuffed animals and other items. The memory of doing the exact same actions after leaving your father was not far from my mind. The way we put ourselves into similar situations over and over while simultaneously thinking we were escaping them never ceased to torture me in its irony. The kennel I transported the cats in while Frankenweenie acted as Chief Navigator on the front console was still set up in the back-cargo area behind the back seats. I called their names, Pete! Larry! and waited, shaking a container of their favorite treats. Pete appeared right away, sniffing at my feet, but no Larry. I shook again, listened, and checked the time on my phone. The possibility that Joseph would return, begging me to work things out, was not far from my mind. All I wanted was to drive back to Colorado and resume a life I had been trying to escape. Florida was no savior, and I found the same problems followed me here that I thought were left behind.

You said nothing as I secured Pete in the kennel, you in your car seat in the backseat, and set Frankenweenie upfront with me as co-captain for our return home. Larry still hadn't shown up, despite my treat box shaking and calling out his name. It never took him this long to come back, ever. I was becoming frantic, panic causing me to hyperventilate as I called Larry's name over and over. He could be roaming the preserve, too far off to hear me, stalking and hunting. I thought about leaving him for a split second, panicking over the time, not able to wait any longer, but I didn't. David Caradine might have been many things, but he wasn't wrong about guilt and responsibility when you save someone, or in my case, an animal's life.

What seemed like hours went by, and Larry came running, an orange dart, towards me from the direction of the preserve. I grabbed him, too much in shock to think how or why, and locked him inside the kennel along with Pete. They had their food bowls, water, and a litter box. As far as a long-distance drive, they were as prepared as they were going to be, and they had already made the same trip out here. Just in case, I sprayed some calming spray over them I got from their vet in Colorado, telling them some quick words of encouragement, then shut the back and locked it.

Sometimes, one end of a connection never finds the other end, and it continues to search until it destroys itself. We made the trip back to Colorado in 37 hours with only one breakdown in Kansas and a blizzard greeting us as we made it back to Denver. I could almost hear Candy, my mentor in maidship, sing-songing to me; your struggles aren't over yet, honey. You got a long, long way to go.

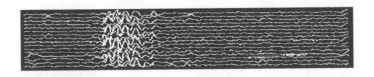

I spread my legs for him, but they weren't wide enough. But the highway between Denver and Florida was. A temporary home. Two cats, one dog, one son. My friends all told me I'd burned my bridges. There was nothing to come home to except a town full of cancer and an empty house.

Tennessee is misty and wrapped in wet. It's a large, yellow bison, not minding the rain. Forests on both sides of the road. Ancient deer that seem prettier in picture books. A smoothness to the highway that feels tight under the wheels of a Jeep. How the rubber grips the road, terrified of losing itself. That was me, maybe him too. I came with too much to be put away neatly. A failed engagement, a son with no father, and hope when there was no reason to. Such an open-ended word. An aging pear waiting to be cut open.

In Florida, everything smells like drugstore perfume. Scents on top of scents. No one is happy unless you're just visiting. I saw the ocean twice, once at night. The waves were purple-black, bruises on the dead (he said), and I couldn't seem to exhale. There's a story behind Hollywood, Florida, about how the founder wanted to name it after his dream city. *This ain't no dream,* Joseph said, but I disagree. Dreams don't always mean something good, I tell him. He eats his tortilla-wrapped *Pulpo A La Parilla,* smacking his lips together. *Why Florida?* But I can't tell him it's the ocean I love, not him. The ocean is a different planet. Me, as a girl visiting my grandparents during summertime. It was a time to discover. Crabs hid under plants, manatees, and wearing purple jelly shoes. So different from the mountains I grew up in. I remember stones under my feet and the feel of warmth brushing against my legs.

I remember a warmth of salt and seaweed and a man shouting my name as his arms cut air, as the water drowned me (away from him).

Be Careful What You Wish For

After I left him in Florida, Joseph posted a picture on Facebook of his hand touching the wedding dress I wore on the beach the day we were married. I left the dress, and him, a ghost hanging in an empty closet. The dress was pearl white with spaghetti straps and more lovely than the photo depicted. With my body inside of it, I became beautiful, wanted. I had a power over Joseph that I didn't have over a man before, not even with Alex. He never stopped wanting me. I became an insatiable need for him, but without any balance. It was as if I had placed a spell on him, and maybe I had—maybe I wanted someone so bad I didn't care who, as long as they wanted me even more. But there was no way to end it. It was all an unheeded warning; *be careful what you wish for.* I stared at the picture as a text from him popped up on my phone.

Can we work this out?

Driving from Florida through Tennessee, I was reminded of the relatives I never knew and would never know, except in photographs. The old farmhouse in Buffalo Valley was overtaken by sea oats and sunbursts. The hills leading to Appalachian bones, away from the ghost town of my pawpaw and meemaw.

I held out exactly two weeks longer than the state allowed for an annulment. The papers were served to his father's house in Deerfield Beach, knowing the house was abandoned, knowing Joseph would refuse the papers to try and win me back. I never wanted to return to Florida. The days of my summers spent there as a child, sitting behind my grandmother on her motorbike and fishing on the tiny, weathered boat, were long gone.

A vicious wind pushed me further along the highway, and I was reminded of the devastation of the hurricanes that hit Florida. My aunt in Tampa told me once of a sacred stone buried a long time ago by the Seminole Tribe long before Andrew Jackson brutalized his path across the territory. The stone was meant to protect people living in Tampa and the surrounding areas. But I didn't believe her. Nothing can save you from destruction if it's already in motion.

Another text popped up from Joseph with only a photo. This time the dress was gone and the closet empty. I felt a familiar ache, knowing I would be alone like I was after Alex left. Knowing the expanse in time between human touch and nothing was an eternity. I could almost justify turning back just so I would never feel lonely again.

The road in front of me stretched ahead, an endless black highway filled with ghost lights and the eyes of deer hesitating along the roadside; one hoof froze in the air, waiting for a safe moment to cross.

Hourglass

After we returned to Colorado, we lived briefly with my dad and stepmom until the stress of it all nearly drove a wedge between our relationship forever. I understand more now than I did back then. Having a child move back home after lying about an engagement to a man in Florida, having it quickly dissolve, then moving back home in less than three months is not a comfortable situation. I had ruined many relationships trying to find love, but with each act of self-destruction, we always had each other. Still, when they approached me about giving up custody of you so they could take care of you, I was floored. I might have been an unstable person, putting us in danger with your father, running, failed relationships, but not once had I ever given up on you. Not once had I ever thought to leave you.

One morning, I loaded all of our belongings into my Jeep, once again, and moved out of their house for good, leaving my spare key on the kitchen counter and locking the door behind me. I was so hurt that my own dad and stepmom thought that I was such an unfit mother that I needed to give up my custody of you to them, reminiscent of how hard I fought for you in the custody trial with your father and the feeling of being in the same category of "unfit parent" as your father made me want to vomit. Still, I knew I had enough resolve to find a place to live and gain my footing again, back in the same town where I was born and raised and had spent so many years of my childhood in. I pulled a Tarot card as I waited inside my Jeep for an appointment to look at a rental, drawing The Sun with all of its hope and light. Maybe Colorado Springs would work out for us after all.

I found a rental house that accepted my unemployment as wages, and Pete and Larry, with a small deposit, and we moved in. I gave Frankenweenie to my uncle, who lived 15 minutes away. His dog of 20 years had just passed, and he was far more stable than we were. Now, Frankenweenie had a permanent home with a huge backyard and an owner who would spoil him. We could still visit anytime we wanted. Our rental was a cute two-bedroom house on the westside of Colorado Springs near downtown. I cleansed the inside first, opened all of the windows, and smoked the entire house out with pine needles from the tree in the backyard. I salted the windowpanes and outside the door, drawing a small sigil of protection, and placed it facing outward from the windowsill near the bottom corner, conspicuous but still visible. I filled a few small bowls with honey and placed them around the house, summoning angels and other protective spirits. We had returned to the city your father still lived in, and even though it was a big city, it was still small enough to run into people you don't want to see. I took a pinch of the salt left in my palm and sprinkled it on my tongue, rubbing the granules against the roof of my mouth with the tip of my tongue. It tasted good after weeks of nothing but Dollar Store packaged food items.

I quickly found a job on Craigslist, delivering food to people from different restaurants around town. The man who hired me worked in a small office he rented not far from us. He handed me a food delivery bag, much like a pizza delivery pouch, and told me if I got a text message from him, I had five minutes to accept the delivery, or he moved on to the next delivery driver and so on. "I don't reimburse for gas, and you keep all of your tips, of course. If you miss three orders in a row, you're out." I nodded and took the delivery pouch from him as he answered a phone call, waving me away.

While you were at school, I accepted five orders and delivered them all around town. I could go inactive on my delivery profile, and I did to pick you up from school. We headed home, which was starting to look more like a home, with a thrift store couch and coffee table, a small card table with plastic chairs where we could eat, and two bed-frames and mattresses I put on my credit card. Our life was a constant repeat of starting over. It seemed we never hung on to anything; possessions, a home, one location. We only had each other. It was both an empty and fulfilling feeling at the same time. Knowing you didn't need anything. Everything was temporary, replaceable. Turning over the hourglass when the sand ran out and starting over again.

Home is Where the Fear Remains

The rental house was perfect, with a rectangle-fenced backyard to play safely and privately. I planted a small garden, but as I was adding up the bills in my head, I knew something had to go; that something was the trash collection because why on top of everything else did I have to pay for trash when I knew I could take our few bags to the apartment complex down the block to their dumpsters and not be noticed. We headed to the apartment complex as the smell of our throwaways earlier that week filled the air. You puckered your lips, pinching your nose, and we laughed as we tried to make a game of it. *How Long Can You Hold Your Breath?* as I parked and tossed, ready to get home, the word sounded funny in my mind, *home*, and even as I was considering the thought of having a place all our own with a garden, a safe space, the man was in my face. His breath smelled like hot bourbon, pointing at the bags I just disposed of, firing words ILLEGAL and COPS as I jumped into my car and slammed the door, cutting asphalt as you screamed, while the man chased after us, while I turned down the wrong road and became lost in a neighborhood I once knew as a child but somehow looked foreign with multi-level houses and garden-yards as we sped down unfamiliar roads with a man in my rearview and I had no way of knowing where to turn where to go where to find our way home.

Rag Doll

We watched the flooding on live news. Tree branches piled, plastic bags, and paper coffee cups bumped into each other, looking lost. The TV showed a woman being pulled out of the drainage ditch. The ditch was down the street from our house. I knew because I recognized the mall in the background. One afternoon I took you along the bike trail that wound along the drainage ditch. You carried the stuffed Dalmatian named *Doggy* I bought you for Valentine's Day. A homeless man sat on the side of the trail and asked for money. You tried handing him your Dalmatian, but he wouldn't take it. Your hands held the dog in the air, and the clouds puffed their way across the sky.

The woman pulled from the ditch was heaving on the side of the trail. Emergency workers surrounded her. She was crying out the name of her son as the camera panned the length of the swollen drainage ditch. ¿dónde está mi hijo? You asked what she was saying, and I told you she asked for her child.

"Where did her baby go?" I took a breath and turned my head to answer. You were pointing your small finger at the television, eyes wide. "She jumped, Mommy!" I whipped my head and watched as the woman's body, a rag doll now, disappeared into the water.

A Single Mother's Spell for Protection

I took an old photo of your father and scratched his bright blue eyes out with a butter knife until they were unrecognizable. His ears and mouth too. I placed the photo in an old Mason jar I found under the kitchen sink. I needed Spanish Moss to confuse and tangle him— keep him occupied, but I had none. I had barely anything in the kitchen or our house. Not even bare essentials. I grabbed a package of Ramen Noodles, boiled and cooled the nest of noodles, then placed them inside the jar on top of the photo of your father. I secured the lid on the jar and spoke words over it to protect us from him.

I spoke words to command him to stay far, far away. I found my voice, and I shouted and shouted until I grew hoarse. Until I was emptied of everything; the memories of him and what may continue to haunt us in our future.
I spoke words I hadn't been able to speak in years.

Next Time, Smile

I took you on the deliveries with me, leaving you in the back strapped in your car seat as I ran to the door to deliver food. Sometimes I was tipped a few bucks, sometimes a dollar, sometimes more. I didn't get tipped at all a few times, just a door shut in my face after the food was handed over. I wasn't new to food delivery. In high school, I worked at the Pizza Hut down the road, saving enough money to buy my first car, then moved into delivering pizzas, where the tips were good, and I liked getting out of the store blasting my music during the drives. I was still familiar with the neighborhoods of my hometown, even having been away for years. The Springs is a mixture of a heavy influence of the military with the overseeing Christian presence of Focus on the Family and New Life Church. People are judgmental and stiff. The junior high I attended had a strong connection to both, and I remembered being in the same hallways as James Dobson's son, who was rumored to jerk off in the back of the class. I didn't blame him. If my father was James Dobson, I'd want to touch myself all the time just to feel something, anything, other than numbness.

There were ghosts from my past living there, and I tried to avoid going out, even to run errands. Your father was everywhere. The hauntings of his presence were felt on every sidewalk, inside every store, and late at night when the motion lights on the front porch of our house were activated. It was a risk I had to take moving back home. We had nowhere else to go. But I am your mother. I had to make decisions for both of us, and they weren't always the best ones.

We hardly had any food, and my unemployment benefits combined with what little I made delivering food plus tips weren't enough to cover all our bills. I still couldn't find a full-time job. Although Colorado Springs is the second-largest city in Colorado, the jobs were scarce, at least the ones I could do with a small child and no one to help watch you during the day. Just as I was figuring out what to feed you for dinner, a text came in for a delivery. It was to a local frat house at the private college downtown, and they always tipped well.

"Let's get your shoes on," I told you, grabbing your sneakers from your room along with a coat.

"No!" You were sitting on the couch in the front room watching SpongeBob from our tiny TV. I tried to coax you into your shoes.

"Once I'm done with this food run, we can get some dinner," I tried baiting you, but you were adamant, raising your feet in the air away from your shoes and screaming NO! I made my face even with yours, so you looked me in my eyes. "Mommy needs money to get food, sweetie. And I can't leave you here alone, understand?" You were no longer listening; eyes turned to Patrick and Squidward on the screen.

"I'll stay here, Mommy. I'll be good." You pointed at the TV and laughed. I considered it. The time to respond ticked away before

I lost the delivery. Before I changed my mind, I told you to stay inside, don't move from the couch, and I would be right back. The college was only a few minutes from our house, and the delivery wouldn't take longer than 15 minutes. It was hours past the rush hour commute. I kissed you on your head, but you weren't paying attention, still fixated on the scenes blurring across the screen. I locked the door behind me and drove off, watching the door to our house in the rearview mirror.

I picked up the food from the restaurant downtown and found the frat house, an old, sagging Victorian house in the downtown area converted into housing for the local college's pledged brothers. There was a party going on, strobe lights, heavy bass, and men sat on the porch and front lawn in plastic folding chairs. I walked past them to the front door, carrying several delivery pouches with me. They ordered seven pizzas and three appetizers. The smell of the food wafting from within made me weak. "Chris?" I asked a tall man loitering right inside the hallway past the screen door.

"Yo!" he replied, cracking the door open for me. He looked me up and down, his eyes resting on my chest, which was hidden under a jacket. "What's your name?" He asked. I ignored him, wanting to get back.

"That's 75 dollars for everything."

He frowned as he grabbed for his wallet in his back pants pocket, his hand pulling out air. "Fuck!" He stared at me, smiling. "Forgot my wallet. Hang on."

I watched as he ran up the stairs in the hallway and heard feet pounding on old wood, drawers opened and closed, laughter on the front lawn. I wanted to be this careless. I was sick with worry and needed the money before I could leave. More laughter from upstairs this time, then a loud crash. Laugh track laughter. A guy brushed past me and walked inside, turning to grin at me.

"You waiting for someone?" he asked, licking his lips.

I told him, yes, for Chris. He shouted his name, and after another agonizing minute, Chris appeared, wallet in hand. He handed me four twenty-dollar bills and told me to keep the change. "Next time, smile." Hot anger, so hot, flashed through me. I wanted to unleash on him why I was there, why I needed more than just five dollars as a tip, how much food I carried, how much I carried every fucking day, but I knew he wouldn't listen, didn't give a shit. I took the money and left.

I heard you crying before I could get out of my car. Running towards the door and unlocking it, keys fumbling, anxiety coursing through me like an injection. I finally managed to unlock the door and found you standing on the couch, face red and wet from tears, sobbing. I ran to you and picked you up, our faces falling together, my cheeks wet. "I'm sorry," I said, over and over, kissing you on your head while SpongeBob laughed his impossible laugh from the TV.

A mother tiger will leave her cubs for weeks to seek out food if it's scarce or to lure away threats from male tigers. Cubs can easily be killed by prey when their mother isn't there to protect them. A mother tiger will fight to the death to protect her cubs, often sacrificing herself.
I have led too many threats off our track trying to protect you.
We are red in a field of white.
I am not a tiger. Not even close.

The Ghost of Paige Birgfeld

My friend Melanie told me about men willing to pay women money just to spend time with them.

"You don't need to do anything. Just hang out with them. You know, show them affection." She said, picking at her freshly manicured nails. I couldn't believe men would pay women, or anyone, to just hang out, and I told her so.

"Men are lonely here, especially military men. Think about the percentage of military men in this town alone, paychecks sitting in their pockets, just waiting to be spent on another lonely night at the bars." She smoothed the curls in her dark blonde hair and met my eyes. "You need money, and you have the time. Just try it, and if it's too weird, then don't do it again."

"Have you done it?" I asked her, still not convinced. I'd seen far too many true crime shows to allow my guard to drop that easily.

"A few times, sure. Listen, what do you have to lose?"

I needed money. I was having a hard time finding work and couldn't afford to pay for daycare even if I did find a full-time job. No one else could watch you. After moving out of their house, I still wasn't in a good place with my dad and stepmom. My mom lived in Denver, over an hour away, and I didn't know where else to turn. The thought of going on dates for money was the lesser of the evil spectrum for me at that point, and although I was fully aware of the dangers that it could lead to, I knew as a woman it was just one way to make ends meet. Still, the thought of putting myself in a dangerous situation and having you lose me was enough for me to focus my efforts elsewhere.

"I can't do that, Melanie. I'm all he has. I have to try to be responsible. Especially after all of the hell I've put us through." It was true. I was convinced it was all good decisions and sound choices from here on out. I tried to convince myself I was an arrow on a straight trajectory, focused and responsible.

I thought about all of the women in the sex industry who had been sexually assaulted and murdered just trying to make a living. How many of those women were in similar situations to my own. The dancers I watched when I went to strip clubs for fun with friends, my hands full of dollar bills ready to secure underneath G strings. How I felt guilty that I was one step away from being on the same side of their fence, yet, still unable to cross. The girls I saw accompanied by older men going into the motels I used to clean, skinny legs wobbling in high heels were all still too fresh in my memory. One woman I learned about from the local news remained with me: The ghost of Paige Birgfeld. As a mother, sometimes you do everything you can to take care of your children, which places you in the path of dangerous men who want and who take and destroy. It's a tragic bond to have with women trying to survive. Who have been assaulted and murdered because of a man's intentions and wants. Their desire to overtake and force and conquer.

Paige lived in the back of my mind since they found her body in Grand Junction in 2007, 300 miles away from me and, at the time, in a familiar situation to my own: a single mother trying to make a living. But during the investigation, police discovered that Paige was living a double life. Having previously worked as a stripper where she met her husband, Paige decided to work several part-time jobs to cover the bills and ensure her children were taken care of. One of those jobs was the creation of "Carrie," a high-end escort on a website called Models, Inc. I can't blame her for her actions. I can't even look at her face in the newspaper articles online, knowing she suffered a terrible end at the hands of a man who tried to book an appointment with Paige–Carrie–but she had repeatedly refused. She told close friends who knew about her escorting job that this man "gave her the creeps." After Paige disappeared, her car was found burning across the street from the business of the same man who refused to take no for an answer and later admitted to killing her. He wanted to own her. Thought he could own her because she was doing what she had to do. The edge she fell over and the one I was facing was the same, and I could feel the pull of gravity wanting to tug me over. Still, she was a warning for me to not place my safety or risk my body in the hands of a stranger. I heeded her ghost and its message.

Denver Public School District

900 Grant Street Denver, CO 80203

INDIVIDUALIZED EDUCATION PROGRAM (IEP)

Legal Name of Student: ████ ● Leftwich		District ID: ████
School of Attendance: Lincoln Elementary School		Date of Meeting: 2/14/2012

☒ Create a new page

ANNUAL REVIEW
Present Level of Academic Achievement, Functional Performance, and Educational Needs

Include statements in all relevant areas including: Educational, Communication, Cognitive, Social/Emotional, Physical Health, Physical Motor, and Life Skills/Career/Transition.

Educational

INTERPRETATION:

████ is a 2nd grader in a traditional classroom. He is showing progress in his academic areas, but his behavior often interferes with his learning. ████ is a very social child, who would often rather entertain his peers than tackle the assignment at hand. This is particularly true when he encounters work with which he is struggling. In a small group situation, it is much easier to get his attention and keep him on task. He will also then ask for help when he doesn't understand something.

████ transferred into Denver Public Schools this year from Cherry Creek Schools. At the time of the transfer he was receiving 15 minutes consultation a week and 90 minutes a week direct pull-out outside the classroom from the Special Education teacher. He was also receiving consultation and direct motor services and consultation for Mental Health services. These totals were accepted with the transfer IEP.

Reading was on grade level with a DRA 16 at the beginning of the year, so consultation has continued in that area. In addition he has been pulled 2 1\2 hours a week for math and has been making progress.

████ is easily distracted and needs constant movement. His teacher, Mrs. Miley reports that he leaves the classroom about once an hour to go to the bathroom or to get water. The difficulty is that he does not necessarily return to the room and sit down to do his work. He will talk to peers, dance/sing, turn cartwheels, or tell fabricated stories to get attention. He is often impulsive and has gotten into trouble for breaking school rules.

RECOMMENDATIONS:
1. Systematic, explicit instruction in reading and math.
2. Reminders to stay on task.
3. Practice and repetition of skills to reach mastery.
4. Use of manipulatives.
5. Preferential seating.
6. Oral presentation.
7. Flexible break schedule with movement breaks.
8. Behavior contracting

Thank You for Sending Us Your Work

We didn't last long in The Springs before I packed what little belongings we had and moved back to Denver. With the help of your grandma, we found a place to live where she co-signed on the lease, a necessary action because of my scattered rental and job history to date. I found jobs, sometimes two or three part-time gigs at a time: working as a private investigator, maid, and a collections agent for the state. As best we could, we became settled and created a safe space for ourselves. You never saw your father again, and he never bothered to ask. Neither have you. Once the courts granted me full custody, they refused to allow him access to you without a year's worth of specialized psychiatric evaluation for violence by a licensed professional and supervised visitation, both of which he never did.

I remember waiting with you in an empty room at a state agency building in Denver, wondering if he would show up while the agent tapped her pencil against her clipboard. You played with Doggie, your stuffed Dalmatian, tossing the stuffed dog into the air and catching it. I stared at the posters on the walls–affirmations of "Good Parenting" gone bad.

It only takes 30 minutes to make a lasting impression on your child.

A good parent doesn't mean a perfect past.

Parents aren't perfect!

After thirty minutes, she allowed us to leave, noting that your father never showed up for his supervised visitation. I knew he wouldn't. He wasn't interested in being your father if it didn't benefit him in some way.

We secured an upstairs apartment in an old Victorian house near South Broadway. It was big enough for the two of us and Pete and Larry, with access to the shared backyard for you to play. Your elementary school was right across the street. You became friends with a boy in your class named Dante and best friends soon after with another boy named Jack. The three of you were inseparable. It was good to see you make friends, knowing we weren't going anywhere. I wasn't going to allow us to. We were there to stay. Denver was our home.

I began to fall behind on bills and discovered that all of the different payday loan companies didn't use the same system, so I took out one payday loan, then another, then another, until I was up to five payday loans to get us by. I paid them off in full before the due date and borrowed again, a constant cycle of borrowing and repaying, just to make ends meet, but the ends never met. They were constantly broken. This system counts on people never being able to get ahead, always running behind. Always running.

On my lunch breaks, I continued to write, this time focusing on writing about you, what it was like being a mother, what we had been through. I'd carry a spiral notebook around with me everywhere, ready to write down any inspirations that came to me. Soon, it became filled, and I kept buying more notebooks.

Once, while cleaning a house, I thought of Lucia Berlin and her book, *A Manual For Cleaning Women*, and felt empowered by her words describing working women. How I, too, could write about cleaning people's houses, scrubbing toilets, and how I often saw what other people didn't. How people hide things behind closets, underneath beds. Secrets they wanted no one else to see. But I did. I saw everything. I wrote about working as a private investigator partnering with criminal defense attorneys, becoming a witness to the sorrows of the darker side of human life. How fucked up our justice system is when it comes to people being profiled. When "innocent until proven guilty" is often ignored when seeking justice. But when I started having to work cases about children, sexual assault, and murder, I couldn't handle it. I thought I was tougher, but the case with a boy your age at the time found dead, and a brutal sexual assault and murder case of a young woman was too much. Eventually, I had to quit to protect my own mental health.

By writing more and more, I began to feel a healing force grow inside me, something I hadn't felt before. I had no one in my life. It was just you and me, and it felt good for the first time since I could remember. I focused on writing, hoping to one day become published, hoping to get a book published, even though that day felt so far away. Writing has always been my sanctuary—a place that lacked judgment—a space where I could write the words I knew may never see the light of day, and it didn't matter. Like a spell, my words manifested what I needed most; security and grounding, filling a hole that only I could fill. No one else. It was something I had just for me, something I didn't have to share with anyone if I didn't want to. It felt secret and safe. A hidden power.

I was exhausted from work and worrying over you, but the words I found when I was writing and the peace it brought me were my life force. I couldn't stop, no matter how tired I was or how many rejections I received after submitting my writing. As time went on, more rejections stacked up. I began volunteering as a reader at different literary journals, determined to educate myself on what it was like to be on the other side of the editor's curtain. It was a motivation I hadn't felt in a long time. After years of being told no and failing, getting a rejection wasn't the worst thing in the world for me. I kept writing, kept reading whatever books I could get my hands on, soaking up each word with a ferocity I had never been familiar with before. I read what other writers I admired recommended. I spent a lot of time at a local book, music, and coffee shop, Mutiny Info Café, off South Broadway. You loved coming with me to explore the local shops and get a slice of pizza or ice cream. The neighborhood's vibe felt comforting to me, people who didn't conform to societal norms, who talked about writing, music, and magick. At Mutiny, I read the new indie press releases. I read poetry I didn't understand, just to taste the words. I read fiction, nonfiction, and experimental forms. I became so completely engrossed within these forms they later became a part of me. Experimental always felt like breaking the rules, bending the norms, and never felt suffocating, something I desperately sought after and continue to, even to this day.

One evening, as I stood in line at one of the payday loan places while you played with your Matchbox car on the tiled floor, wondering what in the hell I was going to scrape together for dinner, I received a notification on my phone.

Dear Hillary,

Thank you for sending us your work. i love this funny little story. it really stands out amongst a bunch of non-standing-out fiction subs in my inbox. :)

i'd love to accept this if it's still available.

please reply either way!
thanks so much.

I stared at the email of an acceptance for a short prose piece about infatuation gone bad, one I had specifically submitted to a journal I loved, and my heart began racing.

"I did it," I said, rereading the email, just to be sure. I scanned for any "unfortunately's" or "although's" and didn't see any. "I did it," I repeated.

"Next," the woman behind the counter called out in a flat tone. I stared at my phone while you tugged at my pants leg. "Mommy," you called up at me, pointing to the counter.

"Next."

"I did it."

"Mommy."

"Next."

I stepped up to the counter where Brenda was waiting for me behind her computer, face aglow from the screen's light.

"I'm getting published!" I showed the phone to her without thinking, my eyes wide, not expecting her to react. But her face slowly changed from neutral to all grin.

"You're getting published? In a magazine?" Brenda asked loudly as I nodded my head so hard and fast it could have rolled right off my neck and onto the floor. "This woman has gotten herself published!" Everyone in line behind me stared as one man began clapping slowly.

"Congratulations!" scattered throughout the room, and I couldn't stop smiling as I pulled out the 530 dollars in wads of 20s to pay off my loan. Brenda took the money, still smiling, and placed the usual stack of papers in front of me to fill out. When I was done, she handed me 500 dollars back.

"Let me know when your book comes out," she winked.

As we headed for the door, we left with a wad of 20s in my wallet and people congratulating me who had no idea what for, but it didn't matter. The fluorescent lights flickered, and the smell of dirty money filled the air as I swung the exit door open, cigarette smoke and the sound of the cars on Colfax Avenue rushing by. Voices called out, and sirens wailed in the distance. I grabbed your hand and helped you to the Jeep, skipping as we left the payday loan building.

"Can we get Wendy's, Mommy?" You asked, and I nodded.

"You can have anything you want tonight, my sweetpea. The world is ours!" I stretched my arms out wide as the men smoking outside chuckled.

"I want your world too, Mama!" they called out, taking long, deep drags off their cigarettes, the cherries burning bright as wolf eyes in the dark.

Nothing could shake me that night. For the first time, I had hope that my words might actually make it in a world full of other words that always tried to silence me. I never forgot that day, even though it took me years to get past the point of payday loans, pawnshops, and paychecks that were always too small and far in-between.

This was the beginning of working towards something more, for you and for me. I always said; the worst anyone can say is no, Son. After being told no for so long, being told yes is such a warm word to hear. I don't ever want to stop working toward yes.

A Spell of Endings and Beginnings

My son:

I want you to know I would rather have you with me than any of the words I have written. More than all of the oceans in the world. Take these words and use them as a starting point for your own journey and explorations. Remember, you are strong and fought hard against death when she came for you. And one day, you will face your own decisions, struggles, and demons. Take these words and build a beautiful life. No one is ever free from sorrow. Make wishes. Take risks. Be scared when it's time to be scared. Be alone with yourself. Remember our adversities and live your beautiful life we fought so hard together to keep. Life and death can't be manipulated, but I'll be damned if they can't be defied.

Should-Be's

The impact of your seizures hadn't entirely made itself known, but issues with short-term memory, information processing, and dexterity in your hands all affected your learning. When I first received your diagnosis, Lennox Gastaut, and considered the loss of the child you were on track to becoming, I mourned that loss. But now, I don't view it that way. You have fought just as hard as I have throughout our journey, maybe even more, in ways, I failed to recognize at the time. As much as I feel this is the story of us, it's really the story of you and your survival. I will never understand how a child can be so strong after growing up in such violence and loss. Maybe I'm not meant to.

I often think of Should-Be Mother and Should-Be Son. Sometimes, as I'm staring out at the backyard of our home in North Denver, your trampoline standing stoic amongst the Russian thyme, I'm reminded of the ghost of the mother I was always chasing, of the ghost of the son I was constantly trying to resurrect in you. Today, we are grounded. I met my partner in life, a fellow writer and a photographer, an advocate for humanity. You never had a dad and never will, but maybe this man in our life is better than a dad. You finally have someone you can look to for guidance who will be your advocate and friend. Someone who understands that the absence of a father doesn't always mean something negative. Sometimes we are better without.

I don't believe I will ever get over the guilt of what happened to you, of the circumstances I put you in because of my dumb, blind faith in someone who only knew how to destroy everyone he claimed he loved. I still don't know what the definition of a mother is (who the hell does?), but I'm learning as I go, as the years go by and you continue to grow. Your seizures have been under control for years now with one medication and with only a few appearances, but nothing like what we dealt with in previous years. No hospitalizations. You're able to do most things every teenager can do, like being cleared to get your driver's license, should you want to. But other activities, like drinking or drugs, could potentially kill you, even as an adult with epilepsy. How even going away for college could be too risky. The world itself seems too dangerous for a child, let alone a child with a deadly storm waiting to form inside his brain. I know to head down the path of what-ifs can drive a parent crazy with worry. But when you've lived on that same path for so long, it's hard to change directions. You have fought just as hard as I have throughout our journey, maybe even more so, in instances, I failed to recognize at the time. As much as I feel this is the story of us, it's the story of you and your survival. I will never understand how a child can be so strong after growing up in such violence and experiences with death. Maybe I'm not meant to.

Homesick

Last year, I finally made it to Seattle. After waiting nearly 18 years, I stood on the beach and watched as the Pacific Ocean spread itself over the rocks beneath my feet. *Fernweh* is a German word used to describe a feeling of homesickness for a place you've never been or could never go. But being able to see the city and the cold green sea that haunted me for so long, no word or words I know have ever been able to capture the feeling as I stood on those sandy beaches dotted with rocks and iridescent seashells, driftwood, and bull kelp strewn about, waiting for the eventual return of the tides to carry them back into the churning waters of the ocean where they belong. There's a longing in me that wishes to be swept into the ocean along with the shells and driftwood that will never fade.

Fernweh. I know this feeling well.

Sometimes, I'll catch a glimpse of *Should-Be Mother* out of the corner of my eye. The ghost of the woman I should have been at one point in my life. But we beat the odds, and we escaped the fate that could have been ours—a time you are unable to remember—memories erased from the seizures that destroyed parts of your brain. But I remember. And one day, you'll read this and know too. You'll read this and hopefully understand that this mother is still here, fighting for you and loving you even harder every day that passes.

If you ever need reassurance, if you ever feel the need to return home: Slow your heart, hold your breath, and one day, you will return to me.

A Note on the Spells and Rituals

The spells and rituals referenced in this memoir are based on books on spellwork, witchcraft, and folk magick I read into my teenage years and early adulthood. In weaving them with the creative elements of the writing, it's important to me to balance both—the spell/ritual itself and tethering them to the words and images. I am by no means claiming to be an expert in any of these fields nor do I insist upon labels. I only know I intuitively felt the most compelled to combine witchcraft and folk magick because that's what worked and felt most comfortable for me. You do you, as they say.

The following books were lovingly read but not necessarily understood by the curious girl I once was in a time when witchcraft was still referred to as "Wiccan" and misunderstood/mislabeled within the New Age movement, especially in Manitou Springs in the 80s and 90s, where I spent the majority of my childhood roaming the streets looking for the magick and spirits that lived there (maybe still do).

Buckland's Complete Book of Witchcraft by Raymond Buckland

Advanced Candle Magic Raymond Buckland

Color Magick Raymond Buckland

Ozark Superstitions by Vance Randolph

American Witch Stories by Hubert J. Davis

The Holy Book of Women's Mysteries: Feminist Witchcraft, Goddess Rituals, Spellcasting and Other Womanly Arts by Z. Budapest

To Ride a Silver Broomstick by Silver Ravenwolf

The Element Encyclopedia of 5000 Spells by Judika Illes

Time Life Books: The Enchanted World Series

The Last Unicorn by Peter S. Beagle

The Egypt Game by Zilpha Keatley Snyder

The Witches of Worm by Zilpha Keatley Snyder

Acknowledgments

Thanks to my family, friends, and writing communities for supporting me. Special thanks to the best writing group on this planet, who helped me with many of the pieces in the memoir: Steven Dunn, my friend and mentor in so many ways. Thank you will never be enough. Thuyanh Astbury, Ahja Fox, Emma Arlington, Brian Lupo, Arielle Roberts, and Meca'ayo Cole. Special thanks to the beautiful writers I admire and took the time and energy to beta read early drafts: Selah Saterstrom, Sarah Schantz, and Jessica Lawson. For those who blurbed this memoir, Steven Dunn, Piper J. Daniels, Sarah Schantz, and Selah Saterstrom, I am grateful to you in ways I can't possibly find words for here on this page. Thank you. To friend and writer Shoshana Surek, who always encourages me. Dustin Holland and Madi Chamberlain for being rad and forces of support in our communities as well as Frankie Met. To Andrew, aka William Seward Bonnie, my Taurus brother forever. To Mutiny Info Café in Denver,

Jim Norris and Charly Fasano who provided me with a safe haven and a world full of books when I first moved to Denver. My neighbor Meghan, who became one of my closest friends and helped watch my son when times were really tough (more times than I can count). To Brenda S. Tolian, my sister in witchhood. To Jaime Turner for being my best friend and writer in kinship, even if we no longer speak. To Chris Caruso. Thank you for not marrying me. It did us both a huge favor.

To Kevin Sampsell, who believed in the earlier draft of this submission to Future Tense Books, sent me a message which got lost in my email and I never saw, and who took the time to message me on Facebook to ask me if I received his response. Who took time and careful attention to the drafts, language, and images. Who understood me when I didn't necessarily make sense, but he knew what I was trying to say anyway. Who talked on the phone with me and got to know me as a human first. Who believes in writers and me and the power of the written word. To Emma Alden, who helped edit and put up with my tenses. To Michael Kazepis, for the wonderful and caring layout design. To Sarah Best, for the beautiful cover collage. To Michael Seidlinger for always supporting me, being a friend, and helping design both of my book covers. To Leza Cantoral and Clash Books for believing in the early drafts of this once-collection of poetry.

The writers who influenced this book: Ocean Vuong, Carmen Maria Machado, Ai Ogawa, Alice Notley, Lucia Berlin, Selah Saterstrom, Sarah Schantz, Piper J. Daniels, Julia Madsen, Faylita Hicks, Mathias Svalina, and Steven Dunn.

To my students: All of you played a part in this memoir. I have learned so much from all of you.

To Stephanie Maney-Wright, my soul sister who never judges me, only listens.

To my partner, Jay, for listening to me read early drafts for hours and days on end and supporting me through the entire vulnerable process of reliving these memories.

Most of all, to my son, the reason why this memoir was written. Love isn't a strong enough word. Hell, is it ever?

HILLARY LEFTWICH is the author of *Ghosts Are Just Strangers Who Know How to Knock* (CCM Press/The Accomplices). Her hybrid collection, *Saint Dymphna's Playbook*, is forthcoming from PANK Books in 2023. She is the founder and owner of Alchemy Author Services & Workshop and is a creative writing professor at the University of Denver and an assistant creative writing professor at Colorado College. She is an intuitive Tarologist and has been reading Tarot for over 25 years and studies under several well-known psychic medium mentors. She lives in Denver with her partner and son.

9 781892 061935